PRAISE FOR THE WORKS OF
CHUCK WENDIG

"A bold, impressive novel with fierce intelligence and a generous, thrumming heart . . . It's intimate and panoramic. It's humane and magical. It's a world-hopping, time-jumping ride that packs a deep emotional punch."

—*Library Journal* (starred review)

"A tsunami of a novel."

—Meg Gardiner, Edgar Award–winning author of
Into the Black Nowhere

"Chuck Wendig's *Wayward* proves that there's always more story to tell. If King had written a sequel to *The Stand*, it might look something like this monumental epic of a story. I don't think I'll get this book out of my head for a long time—maybe never."

—James Rollins, #1 *New York Times* bestselling author of
Kingdom of Bones

"A true tour de force."

—Erin Morgenstern, *New York Times* bestselling author of
The Night Circus and *The Starless Sea*

"A masterpiece with prose as sharp and heartbreaking as *Station Eleven*."

— ~~Shepherd~~ bestselling author of *The Cartographers*,
~~T~~he Book of M, and *The Future Library*

T0286366

"A riveting examination of America—fiction that feels more real than reality itself."

—Scott Sigler, *New York Times* bestselling author of
Ancestor, *Infected*, and *Contagious*

"Only Chuck Wendig can blend horror, fantasy, and science fiction into a propulsive thriller that is as funny as it is frightening, clever as it is uncanny, tender as it is terrifying. A magical ride."   —Alma Katsu, author of *Red Widow* and *The Deep*

"Move over King, Chuck Wendig is the new voice of modern American horror. *The Book of Accidents* is a masterwork, and Chuck is only just getting started."

—Adam Christopher, author of *Stranger Things:
Darkness on the Edge of Town*

Gentle Writing Advice

Gentle
Writing
Advice

HOW TO BE A WRITER
WITHOUT DESTROYING YOURSELF

Chuck Wendig

WRITER'S
DIGEST
BOOKS

WRITER'S
DIGEST
BOOKS

An imprint of Penguin Random House LLC
penguinrandomhouse.com

Trade paperback ISBN: 9781440301209

Printed in the United States of America
3   5   7   9   10   8   6   4

Book design by Ashley Tucker

This one's for the birds

Contents

Two Warnings, Before We Begin xi

Why We Are Here xiii

Something Important 1

1. Two Things You Need to Know 3

2. The Mythology of Process (Or, How I Realized I Don't Know How to Write a Book) 7

3. But Do I Need to Write Every Day? 23

4. But Do I Need to Write Every Day? Part Two! 25

5. Self-Care for Writers 31

Something Important, Part Two 59

6. The Danger of the Myth of the Starving Artist 61

Something Important, Part Three 73

7. The Necessity of Knowing Thyself 75

8. Three True-ish Things 93

9. White-Bordered Optional Stop Signs 103

Something Important, Part Four 131

10. You Are Not Alone 133

11. Genre Is Just Some Shit Somebody Made Up 141

12. When Kids Ask Me for Writing Advice 151

13. The Fine Art of Flinging Fucks
from Your Fuckbasket 157

14. The Joy of Fucking It All Up 167

15. Nobody Knows What They're Doing 171

16. When Is It Good to Feel Bad? A Helpful Guide! 177

Something Important, Part Five 201

Epilogue: You Can't Run on a Broken Leg 203

Acknowledgments and Afterbird 215

About the Author 231

Two Warnings, Before We Begin

1. Writing advice is bullshit, but bullshit fertilizes.

2. This book contains naughty words, like the s-word, the f-word, and the p-word.[1]

---

[1] Publishing.

Why We Are Here

AHEAD OF YOU WAITS A BOOK OF GENTLE WRITING advice. This advice aims to calm the chaotic writer mind, giving you a myriad of ways forward in your storytelling and writing work in an effort to empower you and give you options instead of limiting you with rigor and rule.

And already, I feel you bristling a bit.

After all, you note, I am the person who has offered the following pieces of advice in various blogs and books:

"Art harder, motherfucker."

"Harden the fuck up, Care Bear."

"Stop fucking describing everything."

And, "Get to the fucking story, already."

These are not, you might correctly note, *gentle* bits and bobs of writing advice and in fact might be considered somewhat, um, *aggressive*. My first writing book, plucked from the digitalia of my blog, was called *The Kick-Ass Writer*, for god's sake. One does not kick asses gently. Asses must be kicked aggressively, or they are not being kicked, but rather, they are being *hesitantly toed*, or *carefully prodded*, or *gingerly tapped with the ball of one's foot.*

So, before we get to the question of

Why gentle writing advice?

We first have to answer the question of

Why harsh writing advice?

$$=$$

THOUGH FIRST, A bit of recent history.

Not long ago, someone in the Hell-Realm known as Twitter opted to step in and offer a piece of, as he termed it, Harsh Writing Advice, and this piece of advice exhorted writers to realize that other writers are not your friends, but rather, they are your competition. With that, a great, merciless dunking ensued upon this writer,[1] a poor foolish soul with few followers of his own, because of course the idea that other writers are your competition is a very poor one. Easily disproven. He, unlike many others on Twitter,[2] was wise enough to detect the scent of ozone and fear in the air, and he quickly deleted his tweet before the unholy disk-horse emerged from its dark storm of hot takes to stampede the fellow into human mulch. Still, responses lingered, and I even offered my own initially satirical take on it, suggesting that not only were other writers your competition, but they were your cannibalistic prey, there to be caught and eaten, which is of course how writers steal one another's power. Writers are meat! Hunt them for their hearts and claim your seat at the Author Table! After all, are

---

1　Blessedly not yours truly.

2　Including yours truly.

you even a real writer if you have not bludgeoned a better writer and consumed them for their talent?

It was a joke, of course, as the only test you can take to determine if you're a real writer is this right here:

a. Are you writing?

b. If yes, you are a real writer, congratulations.

c. If no, you are not a real writer, sorry and thanks for playing.

But! I felt like the satire, while funny, failed to actually get to the truth of the thing, and as such, I then offered a new thread designed to serve as counterprogramming to the very notion of harsh writing advice. It was a thread of *gentle* writing advice, there to provide comfort instead of, what? Callousness? Cruelty? I don't know. It just felt right, given, well, *everything.*[3]

But it also had me thinking, What is the value of harsh writing advice? Why did it ever exist? Why did I once give it? And do I disagree with it now?

Why it existed is, I think, an easy question to answer. Once upon a time, as the internet grew legs and began to stumble about like a knock-kneed fawn, most of the available writing advice was, at least to my experience, decidedly *literary*. This isn't a negative, necessarily, just that such advice was less

---

3   "Everything" includes, but is not limited to: Trump, a contentious election, an insurrection, ongoing climate change, a global pandemic, a cascading series of variants and subvariants of said pandemic, and by the time you read this book, who knows what else, probably a city-stomping kaiju or some new rectally invasive spider.

about the journeyman writer, the yeoman, the freelancer, the self-appointed hack, and instead spoke more to the MFA-goer, the author who turned in one book every five years and who spent the rest of their time teaching or doing speaking gigs. Such advice tended to be, for lack of a better term, fairly high-minded, even romantic. Muse-driven. Inspirational and imaginative. It was the kind of advice that was less about getting words on the page and more about listening to the exhortations of the grass and the rain and the clouds. Advice that was often both "artsy" *and* "fartsy." There's nothing wrong with this, really, only that it neglected some of what you might consider *harsh realities* about writing, the kinds of realities that mid-list writers, or genre writers, or even the writers of comics and games faced (and still face) regularly.

These were working writers who had, before now, not been given as much free rein in the realm of giving writing advice—and as such, those writers had some very different advice to give.

And so, once free and clear, they spoke out. They said, wait, no, writing isn't always *literary pontifications* and *listening to birds*; sometimes it's digging ditches, sometimes it's dragging a story out of the clamped-down jaws of an angry wolf, sometimes it's—as the advice often goes—ass in chair, write anyway, regardless of whether you're inspired, regardless of whether or not you feel like it. Writer's block isn't real, these writers said, when you have a mortgage. Take advice from your swooshy Nike sneaker: JUST FUCKING DO IT. I think this advice existed in a way to let people know that writing was indeed work, serious work, real work, as real as anything. Digging ditches is noble, after all. And sometimes what it took to do it was just shedding all of these presuppositions and expectations and just, well, doing it. Writers as movers of earth instead of god-driven spinners of The Imagination.

That tracks for my own career and feelings about writing, too. I began my writing life as a freelancer in the gaming industry. Though there was certainly an art to it, the art was always married to the deadline, to the economy of words, to the essential mercenary mercilessness of however you got words onto the page. It was about writing, yes, but also about scheduling, about discipline, about managing editorial relationships and getting paid. And it felt to me like a lot of what I was experiencing—more to the point, a lot of what would've helped me at the start—was not necessarily reflected in a lot of writing advice. So, with the throaty growl and persistent eye-twitch of a word-war veteran, I figured I'd tell my side of that story.

Of course, everything I said then was wrong.

And, also, it was right.

Which seems, I know, impossible. And yet, here we are, recognizing that many truths exist along multiple axes and they can often exist in polar opposition to one another.

Writing advice is just shit writers made up. It is subjective in the truest sense: true for the subject, and even then, not always, not universally. It's a product of survivorship bias: I DID THIS, AND I PUBLISHED A STORY, THEREFORE YOU SHOULD DO THIS, TOO. Thus, writing advice often ends up being fairly prescriptive—meaning, the advice is there to impose *law and order* onto the chaotic act of writing and storytelling and art-making. Creativity is a lawless land, and art/writing is the act of refining that chaos into order, and so it makes sense in a way that such advice is frequently about the imposition of structure. And artists and authors are often viewed as these wifty, wispy spirits who can't keep it together and who would starve if you didn't press a taco into their searching hands once in a goddamn while.[4] So it's not that I disagree with my early, harsher writing advice. It was right for me then even as it's sometimes wrong for me now.

Certainly my own career thrived on learning the early lesson that if I wanted to do this thing, then that would require work and effort, and that such work isn't always fun, or even pleasant. It meant, for me, ass-in-chair, fingers-on-keyboard. So writing advice I gave back then tended to drift away from the chaotic, unpredictable tangle of writing and storytelling and into the "reality check" style of harsh writing advice—it is often presented as if one is doing a favor by delivering it. "Here," says the author, "is a hard truth someone may not have told you, oh by the way, *you're welcome.*"

Of course, it's not really a favor—nor is it a curse. It's no more important than giving someone directions, say, on how to drive to the beach. Maybe you favor a fast highway route, and so that's how you tell them to go—highways and toll roads. But they'd favor a more ponderous, pokey route in order to see some sights. Writing advice is the same way. There is no one-size-fits-all, and arguably, it's only one-size-fits-one. But we share it anyway, even if it's the "harsh reality check" style. I even think that some part of it is designed to counter advice from charlatans and abusers who want to sell you fake empowerment, or toxic positivity, or shame-based directives. I think it's a way to exhort the notion, "I learned these hard lessons, and most people won't tell them to you, but I will." It comes from a good place. Some people really do need the "hard truth"

---

4 I am certainly able to get my own tacos, but also, I will definitely take any free tacos you want to give me.

approach—again, I did, a decade before now. And I may need it someday soon. So, with that said—

Why gentle writing advice?

Why this book here and now?

HERE, AS I see it, is the problem—

The mode of *harsh writing advice* is in ample, easy supply, and further, it often feels like it's a very masculine style of advice—very Western, very pedagogical, with a lot of stern, grumpy faces and lectern-pounding. BUTT IN CHAIR. FINGERS ON KEYBOARD. WRITE, MONKEY, WRITE. It presents writing as a mathematical equation: as long as we adhere to the formula and plug in the correct variables, we will Properly Compose Content. That is how the work is done. Go, go, go, write, write, write.

But—because ultimately this book is about me more than it's about you[5]—that kind of attitude wasn't working for me anymore. I was in need of counterprogramming. Yes, the *go chip some prose coal from the word mines, you goddamn prole* advice hit me in that sweet spot ten, twenty years ago.

But now, I needed something else.

Part of that was because . . . the world is a rough place right now, with a whole lot of *traumatic miasma* suffusing the very air, and sometimes my place in this world feels tenuous, uncertain, *slippery*. The harsh stuff worked only for so long, for

---

5 The hope is, of course, that you will still find value in it. I can show you the paths I took and maybe one of them offers you a way forward, too. Or at least an interesting view to consider.

when I was a younger penmonkey in a more stable world. That's changed. Things are different. *I'm* different. I've gone around the bend in a lot of ways, and I'm trying to handle myself and the work with a gentler touch.

These are tough times, and creatively, it can become especially difficult to find your way through that tangle of chaos and fear to make art and to write stories. I've found that the last four/five/six-ish years in general have been pretty corrosive to creativity. Certainly for me. Maybe for you.

So maybe if this book is useful for me to write—

Maybe it'll help you, too.

Because this just doesn't feel like the optimal time to say, HEY, HERE ARE THE HARD-AS-NAILS RULES, YOU PIECE OF SHIT, YOU BETTER FOLLOW 'EM OR YOU'RE GONNA DIE. Like, look at it this way: when my kidlet is having A Day™, I can't just pound my fist and growl at him and tell him to JUST GET IT DONE, whatever "it" happens to be. Sometimes you need to sit down and talk him through it, and appeal to him on a human level, a compassionate level, and allow some days to be hard. And on those days where he commits to just doing a little of whatever it is that needs doing, he often goes ahead and gets it all done anyway, because we didn't try to force it. Some things you can't force. Emotions are one of them. And emotions are all bound up in the creation of art and the telling of stories. And for me, this became true—writing got harder, during this time, not easier.

I found my way through it, but not easily. And certainly not by shoving my way through it, endlessly trying to cram a square peg into a circle hole. I had to, well, be gentler about it.

Hence this book.

It's here to tell you that it's okay to take the time you need.

To be gentler on yourself. It's here to help you find your way through the work and not simply be lost in the dark forest. Because I think we need your voice, should you care to share it. Because your voice has value. Your art, your words, have *worth*. They are worth it to you and to the world beyond. So, if you're going to do this thing, there are ways to do it that don't require you breaking your back and bleeding and starving and smashing your nose against the grindstone so hard it turns to a pink paste.

You know, I was once wont to say that writers aren't special snowflakes, but I've come around to believing the opposite is true: We are, in fact, snowflakes. We are unique. We sometimes melt and other times re-form. And when we get together with other writers, we can make a day prettier, we can become a blizzard, we can become an avalanche. There are many of us, but each of us is singular. I think that's pretty neat. More to the point, I'm taking the long way to say that writing is hard, that the times are tough, and that sometimes, taking the gentle way, the slow way, is what works. Especially when the other way doesn't.

Something Important

YOUR CREATIVITY ISN'T A WELL THAT RUNS DRY.
It's an ocean.
It has high tide.
And it has low tide.
But it never runs out.
It has unseen depths—
And rough water.
It contains treasure.
It contains sharks.
Sometimes you just get your feet wet.
Other times, you will be swept away.
But it is limitless.
And you are in no danger of losing it, no matter how you may feel.

1

Two Things
You Need to Know

WRITING IS HARD.

That is the first thing I want you to know.

That I *need* you to know.

Writing is hard.

Stories are difficult.

It's okay. It's not meant to be easy. You're opening up a cabinet of thousands upon thousands of available words, and you're laying those words together, one after the next, sometimes as a layer of bricks, other times as snakes chasing snakes, in order to invent an entire universe full of made-up people and ideas and places, and further, you're trying to line up those people, those places, those ideas, into a cohesive narrative, a story that takes us from the start of a problem to the end of it, a problem that can be as simple as a desire for love to as complicated as wanting to destroy a brutal empire that spans galaxies.

It's hard.

It's *meant* to be hard.

Some days will be harder than others.

And again, that's okay.

I say this, that it's meant to be hard, in order not to scare you off, but also to let you know that on days when it's feeling hard—*that's perfectly normal*. And that's true from the first day of you writing to the last. Even when it feels easy, it's actually hard, because there's always more to do. Sure, other writers make it *look* easy. And that's because the actual mechanical act of writing—often unseen anyway—is just someone hunched over a keyboard,[1] fingers pistoning, making magic with a dance of keystrokes. But the calm surface of that lake hides depths of effort and turmoil and trouble. It conceals all the self-doubt and the uncertainty and the Impostor Syndrome and the fears that you're too young or too old or writing the wrong thing. You look at someone playing a concerto on the piano or building a house and you don't think, "Holy shit, that looks easy." No, you say, "That looks hard," because it is hard, and because those people trained to do that difficult thing. Writing looks easy, but it's no less difficult. It gets easier over time, until it doesn't. Because like in an MMORPG, the moment you level up, it just means you have bigger enemies to battle. It gets more complicated. And some days even simple writing is hard.

You're making universes.

Inventing people.

Mining yourself for ideas.

It's okay that it's hard.

---

1   Seriously, sit up straight. Posture. Ergonomics. Important stuff! It's good for your blood flow, your spine, your digestion.

Sometimes it *has* to be hard.

Writing is hard. Even when it's easy. Even when you love it.

THE SECOND THING I need you to know:

You're going to be okay.

I can't say where the world will be when you read this book. I know where it is when I'm writing it: we're in the middle of a pandemic and caught in the throes of political strife and there exists deadlock on important issues like preserving democracy and preventing climate change, plus I currently occupy a world where chocolate dessert hummus exists, and if that's not proof of a harrowing end-times scenario, well, dammit, I dunno what is.

But the point is, you're going to be okay.

Maybe you can write today.

Maybe you can't.

Maybe you manage to write a lot, maybe just a little.

But the writing is an opportunity, whenever you can seize it. Writing can be a chance for escape. It can be a way to funnel your rage. It can be a place to wrestle with your fears, to contextualize your anxieties, or to do literally none of that and instead enjoy a buffet of vicarious fictional thrills. Writing can help you understand the world outside your door, or it can help you avoid it entirely.[2]

It's also okay to not be okay. This is a deeply absurd, troubled era, and even if it weren't, it is perfectly fine to not be

---

2   Hell, sometimes it can do *both* at the *same time*, that's how cool it is.

perfectly fine. And it's okay to channel that into the work, or to not be able to work at all. Even writing this book has on some days been harder than I would have preferred. Such is the nature of things. Such is the nature of writing.

But the goal is, we persevere.

We hang on to the rodeo bull as it bucks and kicks.

You can do this.

I believe in you.

2

The Mythology of Process
(Or, How I Realized
I Don't Know How to
Write a Book)

CONFESSION: I DON'T KNOW HOW TO WRITE A BOOK.

At this moment, you surely pause, squint your eyes, make a *hmmm*ing sound as you note the obvious: this thing in your hand is a book. And presumably I, the person who just said, "I don't know how to write a book," was the one who wrote this book-shaped thing.

Further, if you have any sense of my career, this is just the latest book atop a pile of, well, *other books*. Between novels and nonfiction works, I've written approximately twenty-five other books at this point in space and time. With more on the way.

This would either seemingly disprove the sentiment that I don't know how to write books, or worse, it might suggest that my books are utter garbage. That they only exist as a publishing version of the Peter Principle, a hymn to mediocrity, that they have failed upward again and again, likely finding homes at publishers and on bookshelves only as part of some grand conspiracy.[1]

Alas, there is no conspiracy.

It's true: this is a book, and I have written many others. Some of them have sold quite well. A few of them have been nominated for an award here and there.

What this means is, I know how to write books.

I just don't know how to write *a* book.

The difference, you ask?

Writing books in general, I get. Like, the overall, "Put words on paper, line them up just so, try to jiggle them into a story shape," yeah, no, I grok[2] that. But individual books? Each their own strange instance of existence?

I don't know how to write this book, or that book, or the next book after it.

And that is a *good* thing.

---

1   And now that you know the truth, I have to kill you. THE INK IN THIS BOOK IS POISON wait but that means you have to be licking it, and are you licking the book? Why are you licking the book? Stop licking books. I mean, unless you really *like* licking books. I shouldn't judge. Also, the ink isn't poison. I'm sorry I said that. It's fine, you can keep reading now. And lick away! No shame.

2   IYKYK. (Otherwise, Google is your friend.) (Wait, that's actually sort of a jerk move, isn't it? Writing a book, then using a footnote to tell you to google something the footnote would otherwise explain? Gosh, I'm sorry. Okay! "Grok" means to understand something or someone, and it is from Robert A. Heinlein's 1961 novel *Stranger in a Strange Land*. Also, did you know his name is pronounced Hine-line? I always thought it was Hine-linn. You learn something new every day. Like that wombats poop cube-shaped poops, or that a cat named Stubbs was once the mayor of an Alaskan town. The more you know!)

The Book That Broke Me

I learned this quite late in my career.[3] Only just recently, as a matter of fact.

See, I *thought* I knew what I was doing. I had a method. I had a process. It was repeatable and, by all evidence, successful. I'd first outline the book. I'd sit down in the morning and write two thousand words a day. I would do this until the book was done. Then, usually, two edits: the first a developmental story edit, the second a copyedit. Certainly there was some slack in the rope in terms of tweaking the formula, but this was generally it. My books were on average somewhere between eighty and one hundred thousand words. I had it figured out.

I was triumphant.

And then came *Wanderers*.

Even at the start of writing that very big book, I didn't have a proper outline the way I usually did; I had, instead, a collection of chapters and character studies. We pitched it on those, and sold it on those, and then . . . oh shit, I had to write the book. I figured, okay, sure, I'll write an outline for this book before I start actually writing, but . . . I didn't? I don't know why I didn't. Some outside force[4] compelled me to just jump in. Into it I went, and my writing schedule was pokey and chaotic. Some days I'd write five hundred words, and I'd feel sad about

---

3   Er, relatively speaking. I've been writing books professionally for ten years and writing freelance for another ten before that. I suppose in twenty years, should I have the fortune of (a) still being alive and (b) still writing books, the revelation detailed in this chapter will have been learned early in my career. Time is funny like that.

4   HAIL SATAN.

that, until the day after, where I'd write three thousand words. And other days I'd need to sit, think, and do research,[5] which meant writing no words at all.

Eventually, my deadline was coming up on me.

I do not miss deadlines.

I don't whiff.

I came up on freelance, and part of how I kept getting free-lance work was, I did *not* overshoot deadlines. I was an archer; they were my bull's-eye.

I NEVER DO IT NOT EVER—

Uhhh. Except.

Except.

There I was, with this book hanging out at a not-so-lean 180,000 words, closing in on my deadline, and being . . . ennnh, nowhere near the end of the book. I mean, we're talking *miles* away from it.

Which, y'know. *Fuck.*

I was one week till deadline. I concocted a plan and contacted my editor,[6] and I said, "I have an idea." And I outlined for her the plan to do a time jump in the book, to leap ahead to the final act of the story, to write it over the next week, and to still get her the book—*boom!*—right on time. Deadline met. Harmony achieved. The grand universal convergence would remain in alignment and the planets would not go spiraling into one another, causing galactic catastrophe.

And my editor's response was, and I'm paraphrasing here:

---

5   Also known as, "Meander around my yard, beseeching birds for their advice."

6   The truly astonishing Tricia Narwani, at Del Rey.

"What? No, don't do that, you tremendous jackass."[7]

And I said, "But the deadline! I don't miss those! And besides, obviously this book is way too leggy already, I need to speed it up." Up until that point, most of my books were written with what you would normally describe as "thriller pacing," meaning, every chapter is a tense sprint, a short sharp shock to the reader's brain and heart.[8]

She said, again, "Do not do that."

My editor told me not to hurry. She said *take your time, go at the pace the book demands, it'll be done when it's done*. And *no thriller pacing*. She said *this book isn't a thriller, so don't write it like a thriller*. Implicitly, I think I knew that? But I didn't know it *out loud*. I wasn't conscious of it. Just hearing this advice made me clench up internally, like I was a collapsing star folding in on itself in a gravitational well of ruined instinct. Every part of me was sure that this couldn't be the way, that I wrote books a certain way, that I finished them on time, and if I didn't do that with this book, then what? Was I wrong about who I was? Would the book be terrible? Did I even know anything about this career I'd chosen for myself? Should I quit? Would I make a good longshoreman?[9]

Still, I calmed my *inner maelstrom*. I gently shoved all my beliefs about myself and my writing process into a drawer, then nailed it shut like a casket.

And I got back to writing.

———

7   Okay, she probably didn't call me a jackass, as she's very nice.

8   Like narrative cocaine!

9   I don't even know what a longshoreman is, or does, so probably not. Do they make short shores into long shores? Maybe they just stand on long shores and stare out at the sea, lamenting at how long this shore is, man.

I took my editor's advice. I went at the pace the book demanded. And I wrote to the ending.

Which is to say, I added on another 100,000 words.

At 280,000 words, it was *the biggest book I'd ever written*, by more than double.[10] We edited it in stages, not one, not two, just a series of rolling edits—nothing huge, but lots of tweaks, nips, tucks. The story remained the same, and ultimately, the word count did as well. It was all for tightening, accentuating, sharpening. Then it was done, and one day, it landed on bookshelves.

That book earned me the best reviews and sales of my career thus far.

A book that broke me. A book I didn't know how to write.

Huh.

When the Counsel We Give Fails Us First

Let's change gears for a moment.

Let's ask this question and see if there's an answer:

Why do writers give writing advice?

I understand why writers *want* it—the art and craft of writing, combined with the business around publishing, is a thorny snarl in a dark forest, and we're just looking for someone to hand us a light and a machete.

But why do we *give* it?

The easy answer is, writers want it, and so we seek to answer the questions posed. Cynically, some writers then charge

---

10   Prior to that, I believe the longest was *Zer0es*, at 130,000 words.

money for that advice, arguably as I am doing right here, right now, with this very book.[11] And yet, I think sometimes we're compelled to give advice, often for free, sometimes unasked for—and I don't necessarily believe this comes from a bad place. I suspect we are ultimately aware of the thorny-snarl, dark-forest problem and really *do* want to leave our flashlights and machetes out for other writers. We think, okay, *we* somehow did it. We cut a swath through. It was messy. It was rough. I lost an eye! A friend fell into a hole and was eaten by pigs. So we want to, as Yoda said, "Pass on what you have learned."[12] Writing advice is just us sharing our wisdom.[13]

That said, there's a dark side to that, too. There exists a thing called survivorship or survival bias, and when it comes to the giving and receiving of writing advice, it's ultimately saying: "Hey, I did these things and was successful, so to be successful, you must do these things." In this way, we codify our process as less a menu of artis-

Different people are suited to different paths.

tic options and more like a formula or program. Other writers want the map, so we draw it for them and say, "Here's the map." We neglect to see, however, that the map we gave them is woefully out-of-date and became out-of-date the moment we drew

---

11   To my credit, I have given decades of free writing chat at my blog, *Terribleminds*. Also to my credit, I have a mortgage. Also, I'm a monster. Which probably isn't to my credit, but here we are.

12   Though shouldn't it have been, "What you have learned, pass on?" Or even, "What learned have you, pass on?" Yoda, you tricky little goblin, you could speak in human syntax this whole time? I bet Yoda was just fucking with everybody.

13   Please insert vigorous air quotes around wisdom ("""wisdom""").

it. We took our path up the mountain, but weather washed it out. We dug a tunnel, but accidentally detonated it behind us. The trail is gone; the cave has collapsed. We fail to see, further, that different people are suited to different paths—someone with stronger legs might be able to climb more directly, whereas a less-skilled hiker might take a slower, more ponderous path.

The truth is that writing is a squiggly, fiddly, wiggly thing. It's not IKEA furniture. You don't just assemble the pieces of pressed particle board and use Allen wrench #479 to connect it all, and ta-da, you've built a Sjarnfblörgen Spoon Cabinet. Art is fire and chaos. Stories have patterns, but few guaranteed formulas. You can't just plug-and-play—this isn't an equation in search of solved variables.

So what works for me won't work automagically for you. What works for you probably doesn't work for me, either. Maybe one part of it does, and that's useful enough—and as long as I don't treat your advice like gospel, that's fine.

Problem, though: we start to treat writing advice like gospel. Sometimes because it's *sold* as gospel.

We hear it, we assume it must be true. So we implement, and if it fails us, the failure feels like *ours*, not a failure of the advice or the advice-giver. And the advice-giver is in no way immune to this effect, either, and here's where I round the bend to the larger point:

We start to huff our own fumes.

We get high on our own supply.

We begin to treat the advice we give as gospel, not just for other writers, but for *ourselves*. We take in a process—a process born of survivorship bias—and make it Our Process. It becomes rule. It's law. It's *dogma* now.

Writers mythologize their own processes. It becomes part

of the folklore we tell about ourselves. "Oh, I get up every day, I have to have my French press coffee, ha ha, then I eat a high-protein breakfast, and soon after I make sure to listen to ASMR podcasts while hunting an elusive Black Goat in the woods, and I tackle the Black Goat and sacrifice the diabolical beast on the Dread Stump. Once that's complete, I put my butt in the chair, refer to my dutiful outline, and write two thousand words before noon, and that's how I write books, always and forever. All Hail the Dread Stump."

But—

But.

What happens when your process fails you?

What happens when the menu of steps and tasks and triggers ceases to be reliable and it does not yield the results that seemed once oh-so-repeatable?

It's like having an active relationship with a deity, and then one day, that divine being is gone. No entreaties answered. No echoes from the canyons, caves, and clouds above. Just a howling void.

Listen, trust me when I tell you: it's harrowing when that happens. When *Wanderers* rolled around for me, and it was stubbornly refusing to do what I wanted it to do, in the way I was accustomed, I thought, Well, that's it. I had a good run.[14] But here was a book that would not be tamed. My process was

---

14 Did I, though? WAIT, you know what, no, I'm not going to do that. This is a book about gentle writing advice and goshdarnit, I'm going to be gentle with myself as well. Yes, I did have a good run. I wrote two dozen books in ten years and I have no intention of stopping now, and *even if I had to stop now* because, say, I was gored to death by a randy elk or I became Elon Musk's enemy and he secretly launched me into deep space as revenge, I did in fact have by nearly all standards a *good run.* Yeah. Eat shit, self-doubt!

dead. I was in free fall. I had no true north; I was just a spinning creative compass, wildly whirling about, unsure what to do next, or how even to proceed.

Lessons Relearned

Thing was, I'd learned this lesson before.

I simply forgot, because my brain is like a rat-chewed shoebox.

Way back when I'd started trying to write novels, I'd written five so-called trunk novels—trunk novels in the truest sense, because they should literally have been remanded to a lead-lined trunk and buried six feet deep in my backyard, lest their *toxic vapors* poison any reader who should accidentally come upon them. They were not merely bad. They were heinous, writhing things—slick, gassily hissing worm-piles of unmitigated narrative feculence.[15]

But then I . . . nnnnyeah, kind of hit rock bottom and decided I'd been chasing someone else's idea of what a Chuck Wendig novel should look like. I was chasing both the idea of what a BESTSELLING NOVEL would look like while also chasing the voices of other authors I'd read and enjoyed—but none of those felt like something that came from *me*. Thus, *fuck it*, said I, and opted instead to write the bitter, mad little book of my heart. I chose to throw out all conventions and rules and supposed precepts of writing—I started to write this book, *Blackbirds*, about a young woman named Miriam Black who can see how you're going to die by touching you. She

---

15   Shit. They were shit.

would be unlikable. She would be profane. It would be written in present tense, third person. It would open in a way considered anathema: with the protagonist regarding herself in the mirror.

It was working pretty well.

Until it didn't.

I couldn't finish it. It wasn't that I didn't have the will—I was young, I was like a sprinkler system of pure liquid spite, eager to Prove Literally Everybody Wrong Somehow. I was ready to rock. I just couldn't muster a complete story. It's like, you ever go into a room in your house and you don't remember why you went into said room in the first fucking place? Yeah, that was me with this story. I'd get about 75 percent of the way through it and the whole thing would simply unspool, like a ruptured testicle.[16]

I did this for about five years.

So, at the end of my rope, I did what any bewildered, failed novelist would do—

I entered and won a screenwriting contest.[17]

The prize for said contest was a year-long mentorship with a wonderful screenwriter named Stephen Susco (*The Grudge*, *The Grudge 2*, *Red*, *High School*, etc.). His specialty was taking pre-existing material and translating it to the screen. My not-so-secret secret goal was to take my unfinished novel to him, have him help me with the story by writing it as a screenplay,

---

16 I hate to be the bearer of bad news, but that's how it would happen. Unspool. Testicles unspool. I know. It's science. This may not be gentle information, but I believe truth is a guiding light.

17 I often say that we burn the map after we draw it. Every writer has their own completely bizarre way into the industry. Chaos reigns.

then I'd just run away with that screenplay and add a bunch more words to it and turn it back into a novel.

He said he'd help me do exactly that.

But then he said, well, first thing to do was to outline the story.

Outline it.

Out . . . line it?

I said, ha ha, no no, Mister Hollywood Man, maybe outlining is what you *Screenwritery Types* do, but here in the shining city of Novelopolis, we do things a little *different*. We listen to the clouds. We whisper to the grass. We become horses and thunderously gallop our way across a windswept meadow, chasing the story down the way a hunter of yore would harry their prey.

His response: "How's that working out for you?"

Touché, Mister Hollywood Man. *Tou-goddamn-ché.*

So! I endured the training montage of running up a snow-covered hill, punching frozen beef, biting a leather belt—all as I took two miserable days to crank out an outline. It was hell. I hated it. I was like my then-infant son when it came time to give him a bath: thrashing about, as if covered in fire ants.

But I did it.

Outline, completed.

At which point it was as if the clouds did part and a spear of sunlight did affix this outline to the world. Angels singing in a holy chorus and all that. Because suddenly, I had a story. A whole story. *With an ending.* It did not disintegrate at the three-quarters mark! Holy crap! Sure, okay, I hadn't yet written it into *novel form*—I hadn't even written it into screenplay form.

But there was finally something there. Finally, a story to tell. Beginning, middle, end.

As designed, I wrote it into a screenplay, then used that screenplay as an outline to boost into a novel, and long story short, that was the book that got me an agent, got me a book deal, and ostensibly launched my writing career.

In interviews, I get asked sometimes, "Are you a *plotter* or a *pantser*?" Meaning, do I outline, or do I just leap boldly into the chaos of the unformed story? Do I plan and scheme, or fly by the seat of my pants? And I tend to answer, based on this experience, "I am a pantser-by-heart, a plotter-by-necessity." Outlining was an act I hated, but I felt I had to do it, that it was an essential part of my process.

When your process fails, change your process.

Here's the thing, though: I have told this story many times. Often at writing conferences, sometimes as part of a keynote speech. And afterward, I started to detect that the lesson I was giving was the wrong one. Because people would hear this story and they'd say, "Ah, this means I too must outline my books."

But that's not the lesson.

The lesson is this:

When your process fails, change your process.

That's it.

My process was failing me. It was not getting me a completed book, so I had to change my process to write that book.

I learned this lesson so early, and then . . . promptly lost it. Or, rather, I got it wrong and took the wrong-headed lesson that OUTLINING IS MY ONLY WAY FORWARD, and then I carved that inaccurate lesson into stone and carried it down the mountain and handed it to, well, myself. It became part of the mythology I told about myself, and so when that mythology failed me—when my process became uncertain and the way forward looked different—I didn't know what to do.

Wanderers challenged me. I didn't outline it at all. And I didn't outline *Dust & Grim*. Or *The Book of Accidents*. I may outline again, I don't know.

Thankfully, I recognized that writing is a river, and sometimes you have to let it take you away. Sometimes you move the waters, but other times, the waters move you. I knew how to write *books*. I just didn't know how to write *this* book, *Wanderers*, and that was okay. Because as it turns out, every book is its own beast and will be tamed in whatever way it so requires. Not only is every book different, but you the writer are different when you start a new book—and you are different still when you end it, before the next one. We are changed by each book. We're changed by the books we write, also the ones we read, also the authors we meet, the people we encounter, the experiences we have. We are changed by *life*. And so it stands to follow that the ways we do things will change with us. They must. We cannot create folklore about ourselves. We mustn't become hidebound in our processes. What works today won't work tomorrow, and that's entirely okay. In fact, I'd argue it's how it's supposed to be. Who wants to read a story that is the same as the one before it, that was forged in the same kiln, poured into the same mold?

> *The ways we do things will change with us.*

Sometimes you walk to work a different way, and you see new things, and that's pretty awesome, even though you risk maybe getting lost here and there.

I don't know how to write a book.

And that's okay. Because you probably don't either.

3

But Do I Need to Write Every Day?

NO! NOPE. YOU DON'T.
Next question?

4

But Do I Need to Write Every Day? Part Two!

UGH, OKAY, *FINE*, YOU WANT MORE OF AN ANSWER than that. I'm picking up what you're laying down. I'll feed you, my baby possums.[1]

One of the core, critical pieces of writing advice you will hear from authors across the spectrum is, as I noted earlier: butt in chair, do the work. And that is amended with: *do this every day*. Write every day. You must. Or you'll, I dunno, forget how to write or never finish a book or explode in flames or fall down a hole and *then* explode into flames.

And once upon a time, I subscribed to this exact piece of advice myself. As described earlier, it became part of my *process* both in practice and in the folklore I crafted about myself. Anyone who would come up to me and ask, "How do you do it? How do you write so many books?" would get the gruff old answer, *Well, my wide-eyed, innocent friend, untouched by the world's many harms and untested by its rigors, I sit my butt in the chair and I write every day, two thousand words a day, in fact, and I do*

---

1   Unless you're Jeff VanderMeer, who is a baby raccoon.

this on the best days and on the worst days, never fail. I would say this, presumably, whilst idly chewing on the stem of a meer-schaum pipe[2] and rocking on a porch chair as a wizened gun dog slept at my feet.

(I am wearing a fancy hat in this scenario.)[3]

And the reason I subscribed to this piece of very pre-scriptive advice was that, as a Young Writer, Wet-Around-the-Neck,[4] I had very little discipline to get the words done. It was only once I began writing in a freelance manner, with dead-lines lining up like a firing squad, that I had to get my ass in gear and commit words to paper quickly, regularly, on sched-ule. It stopped me from falling behind. The rigor of it helped me build intellectual muscle. And by writing a lot, I was learn-ing a lot. Learning a lot about how to write, and about myself as a writer.

It was, in a sense, like exercise. The goal is to exercise not simply when you feel like it, or when some Musclebound Muse moves you to, but rather, on a schedule. Keeps you healthy, keeps you practiced.

Now at this point I suspect you're saying, "But wait, didn't you just say I shouldn't write every day? Now you're saying I should? I AM CONFUSED, NAY, BEFUZZLED."

Hold on now.

When I was *young*, I had to write every day.

It did me a world of good.

---

2   Worry not, the pipe contains only bubbles.

3   I will let you mentally decide what hat I am wearing. But may I recom-mend a homburg?

4   I don't think this is a real phrase, but it should be. Let's get it into com-mon usage.

If you are young, or maybe not so young, maybe just starting out—then it could do you some good, too.

But here's also the thing: I wrote every day, and I built a career in which I was writing or editing something like four or five books *per year*. And wow, *who could've possibly foreseen this*, I started to burn out. I wasn't just burning the candle at both ends. I was chewing the thing from the middle like a starving dog who had no qualms about eating a goddamn candle. So I eased off the throttle and slowed down. I now write roughly one book per year,[5] and it feels better. It doesn't feel like I'm trying to destroy myself. The time of that pace, that schedule, is over. It worked until it didn't. As many things do.

So the real answer to the question, *Should you write every day*, is:

I don't know.

Maybe it's your thing. Maybe you need it. Maybe that pace will kill your excitement of it. Maybe that pace *is* the excitement of it. Maybe it's like exercise for you; maybe it's not. Maybe it's like a day job for you: it's about showing up and putting the words on paper five days a week. I don't know. That's the reality of writing advice: I can tell you only the things that worked for me, and I can tell you when they stopped working for me. I could give you an easy answer, but the easy answer would be a lie. The difficult answer is: you have to find your own pace. Your path is your own. I can only tell you the options.

You have to find your own pace.

Some writers hang their hat on it being part of their process, and thus it must be part of *your* process too, but that's

---

5   Two if I'm nasty.

nonsense. Writing every day is a meaningless metric. A day is a day is a day, and an individual unit of twenty-four hours is not significant in the grand scheme.

Maybe you can only write on weekends.

Maybe you can only afford one week a month to write.

Maybe you do write every day, but only for fifteen minutes here, fifteen minutes there, just a few hundred words.[6]

Maybe you snatch erratic time snippets from the jaws of the chronobeast,[7] writing bits on your lunch break, or when the baby finally decides to nap, or in the fifteen minutes before everyone else in your house wakes up. No schedule, just frog-hopping from temporal lily pad to temporal lily pad.

It's all okay.

The point there is, it's not about the schedule. It's not about the frequency. It's all about whether or not you're writing. Even a little bit. Progress is progress. Doing is doing. Take yourself and this thing seriously. Don't worry about what other people tell you to do. They don't know your life. You don't owe them anything, and your process doesn't validate theirs any more than their process validates yours. The only thing that validates

> *It's all about whether or not you're writing.*

---

6   I've talked about this before, but I will reiterate here: If you write 350 words a day, M–F, weekends off, you will write 1,750 words per week. If you do this for one year, steadily, slowly, you will end up with 91,000 words, which is just above the average novel length. So that tells you how a little bit of gentle, forward momentum will get you a completed novel in one year's time. Given that most writers write a novel once every never, that's pretty legit. You can proceed carefully, easily, and still move mountains. So go move some mountains.

7   Please look for my new novel, *THE JAWS OF THE CHRONOBEAST*, coming from Terribleminds Press in April 2033. It is book one in a decalogy!

your process is whether or not it is producing words on the page at a pace that satisfies you.[8]

You can do this at the pace *you* set.

You must approach the work in a way that suits you and does not break you.

Which brings us to a much larger question—

And that is the question of *self-care*.

---

8   And admittedly, your deadlines, if you have those.

5

Self-Care for Writers

I AM A PROPONENT OF SELF-CARE FOR WRITERS.

I mean, okay, I'm a proponent of self-care for everyone. Humans, dogs, dolphins, robots—hey, be kind to yourself. The world won't always be kind to you, so it behooves you to seek self-care when you can. Even though it goes against our instincts, we adjust our oxygen masks first because we need that oxygen to help others.

And the writing life? The publishing world? Definitely not a realm of pure kindness. The writing life isn't cruel to be cruel, but there exists a lot of *ambient cruelty* built into any system based on envisioning art, producing it, and trying to earn an audience for it. Further, writing is an often isolated and isolat-*ing* act—you're planting yourself in front of a notebook or computer and writing one sentence after the next for weeks, months, maybe even *years*. And then once you've finished that part, you're holding it out, asking the universe to love it. No one part of this is actively or personally cruel, but it can sure feel lonely. It can feel desperate, too. It's easy to lose focus and lose hope—and it only gets worse when someone (agent, editor, audience) takes that story you've worked on forever and tells you, "Meh. *Nah.*"

It's soul-crushing. Heart-pulping. Happiness-*destroying*.

So we take steps to try to protect our hearts from being turned into rancid pudding.

We practice self-care.

What does self-care for writers look like specifically?

It can look like rewarding yourself for the effort. I think some writers assume that the reward of writing is in publishing but aahhh hahaha aahahahhaha ahahahaha ahahahhahaah-HAHAhahahah bwaaaahwwaamwaaa ha ahaaamwaaa haaaaa-hah hah ha[1] ahem yeah no not so much. Viewing publishing as a reward for writing is like viewing fighting a dragon as a reward for getting through a dungeon. Publishing is the boss battle in this video game, okay?

No, by rewarding yourself I mean recognize that writing is challenging, that writing takes work, and that you should be compensated for that work. That means when you're not be-

> *Compensate yourself with whatever it is that keeps you going.*

ing properly compensated yet, you compensate yourself with whatever it is that keeps you going: a self-five, a cookie, a day at the beach, whatever it is that pushes the RELEASE OXYTO-CIN button in your brain. It's like how when a dog does anything good, you give it a treat. Hey! You wrote words. You did good. Go have a piece of chocolate.[2]

---

1   AHAHahahahAhahahahaAAAHAAHAAAAAAHHHHHHHH.

2   And eat it over the bodies of your enemies. Hey, whatever, vengeance can be part of your reward, too.

But it doesn't have to be so basic, either. I think self-care can mean not wading into social media if it is toxic to you. I think it can mean not reading reviews of your work, because that way lies madness. I think it can mean not just seeking pleasure or avoiding agitation but taking good care of yourself, too. Yes, eating chocolate once in a while is fine, but so is eating some nice, healthy protein, and so is taking a walk or going on a run or whatever. Self-care can mean treating your body like— well, if not like a temple, then at least like a really nice Target. More to the point, your body is, in a sense, a machine.[3] One must perform upkeep to keep the machine fed and lubricated with the right fuel. So attending to one's body and one's health is a form of self-care, too.

And of course, self-care means being aware of your rhythms, your schedule, and the needs not just of your body but also your mind. If you push too hard, too fast, you might pop an emotional, intellectual gasket. Certainly someone here is already feeling the urge to disagree a little, that it is far easier to push oneself too far physically than mentally and/or emotionally, but I call bullshit on that. Writers spend a whole lotta time in our own brain- and heart-spaces, and we can definitely let those spaces go feral and wild, or worse, we can exploit their resources and strip-mine them for the work, pushing ourselves too far, too fast. If we are to collectively agree that making art and telling stories *is in fact work*, then we must take writing as seriously as any other effort. I know many writers who pushed too hard, who burned

We must take writing as seriously as any other effort.

3 A machine made of blood and goo!

out. I did. It's a real thing. You need to be aware of that, and self-care means knowing when to pull back from the precipice and not run your emotions into the ground. Because when you do that? You won't work at all. You won't be able to—or won't want to.[4]

But, *but but but*, as with all things, there is a big neon caveat buzzing and blinking in your window as you try to sleep.

Self-care can become something of an excuse, too, can't it? It can manifest as something uniformly good, something that is necessary and productive always in every form—think of how, say, doing research for a book or worldbuilding for a story becomes a task that goes on forever. It feels like progress. It *feels* like you're a real writer doing real writing, because those two things, research and worldbuilding, may very well be necessary to the tale you're telling. But if they're also the things that prevent you from actually telling the story, then they *aren't* productive. They cease to be avatars of progress and instead are limitations. They've gone from being useful tools to anchors keeping you moored.

Self-care can do this, too. You take a day off. Then two. Then a week goes by and you tell yourself, *Well, this is self-care, I don't want to push*, but eventually, you've self-cared your way into not writing at all, ever. In this case, the self-care has

---

4   It's worth noting here that writers of every variety often cannot easily dial back the work, because they have bills to pay, and as it turns out, The Powers That Be really don't like it when you fail to pay their precious bills. They get rather uppity about it, in fact. Being able to slow down and pull back on the work is a privilege and luxury and it must be said that not every writer can afford that. In that case, self-care becomes very much about mitigating the stresses of such a hard-charging wordmonkey life—trying to find joy and pleasure and to de-stress as much as you can, when you can, while still chipping ink down in the ol' word-mines.

crossed a line. It has gone from being a kindness to yourself to becoming an *un*kindness—because if what you really want to do is write, then eventually, you have to write. The work must be done. Making art and telling stories are generative, pyro-clastic, and agitative processes, and by their nature both challenging and conflicting. And putting that work out into the world is a process filled with trial and tribulation. You must be cautious and careful with yourself during all this, but not so cautious and careful you fail to do it at all.

Self-care is not avoiding the arena entirely. Self-care is going in with the best sword and strongest armor you can muster. It's about going into the fight trained and rested and ready.

Or, maybe it's like telling someone how you feel—there is always emotional danger in exposing your heart to anyone. But you know when it's worth it, and when it must be done. Otherwise, all you've done is cloistered yourself until your inevitable end. Writing is the same way. You have to put yourself out there. You have to commit to the work. But you don't have to destroy yourself to do it. There can be gentleness in unison with urgency. There can be a way to hold yourself accountable without giving in to shame. It isn't all one thing or the other.

> *There can be gentleness in unison with urgency.*

The difficulty of the thing is finding the balance between the sharp rock in your back urging you to move, and the pillow under your head urging you to rest. Move, move, move, versus rest, rest, rest. Urgency versus solace, get-up-and-go-go-go versus hey-cool-your-damn-jets. Comfort and discomfort, battling for supremacy. The balance is in knowing when to be urgent, when to burn some fuel and bust your ass—but then knowing too when to relent, when to ease off the throttle for the safety of the machine, to know when you've pushed too hard and you might set the whole thing aflame. It isn't really move *or* rest. It's both. Do one, then the other, then the next again.

How do you know when to go and when to rest? Being in tune with your own rhythms and vibe helps a lot. If you're feeling down or sluggish or headachy or burned out, it's time to rest or take it slow. When you're feeling up, when you're feeling eager and motivated and ready, you go. If there's a point where it feels like you're resting too much, push a little bit harder. Not so much that you snap like a sprig of asparagus, but enough that you've done something, that you've set words onto a page. (Writing can be a game of inches, not miles.) If you're feeling burned out or run ragged, well, it's time to slow down or stop entirely. It's like driving a car, except you're the car.[5] Accelerate when the light is green. Slow when yellow. Stop when you see red.

Self-care is an organic package.

Self-care is *and*, not *or*.

Further, treating yourself and your work seriously *is* a form of self-care. It may not seem like it—we often couch self-care only in terms of comfort and luxury, but also being real about what you want and going after it is very much a way to care for yourself. Making time for the writing? That's self-care. Carving out a place to do the writing? That's self-care, too. Saying that you are a writer because you write, and owning your

---

5   YOU ARE A GLORIOUS, GLEAMING FLESHMACHINE. A MUSCLE CAR IN THE TRUEST SENSE: WET AND PULSING AND FULL OF BLOOD wow I'm really sorry for this.

desire to do this thing—be it professionally or not at all—is empowering. And empowerment is self-care, too, dammit.

Kindness to yourself isn't just about having a piece of chocolate or taking a day off. It's about commitment to yourself and your wants. It's about clearly seeing those wants, and further, seeing them as valid—and then pursuing your satisfaction and happiness in that regard relentlessly, with neither shame nor abandon. Being good to yourself is saying, "This is important to me, this matters, and so I am going to do it, no matter what anyone else wants me to believe."

But that can also be emotionally fraught. We put a lot into this. And that makes us vulnerable.

=

WRITERS ARE NOT a well-protected species.

Emotionally, at least, we are very much hermit crabs in search of a shell—each a weird little vulnerable crustacean crawling their way across the beach seeking both armor and a home, hoping they luck out before the Gull of Disdain and the Plover of Obscurity find them and gobble them right up.

Think back to those grade school Valentine's Day events where you had to scribble together a series of paper heart valentines to drop in the cardboard mailboxes made by your classmates, and all you hoped for was that they welcomed your valentines and gave you one in return. Writers are this, in many ways: we're asking you to love our paper hearts and give us yours in return. Except sometimes it's also our real heart we're giving out, red and squishy. And we're really, really hoping you don't take this opportunity to lock eyes with us and slowly stab it with a sharpened pencil, whiiiiich oh okay you're already doing that, never mind.

It can be kind of a hard gig. People don't think it is. They think it's easy-breezy hug-and-squeezy, just a life of literary leisure and creative comforts. But we are constantly sending out our paper heart valentines to agents and editors, to crit groups and beta readers, to the readers and fans. Rejections abound. Hearts torn in twain, stuck to our lockers with the glue of blood. And rejections can come at any level. An agent invests, but an editor doesn't. An editor buys, but the audience doesn't. The audience buys, but the reviews are terrible. The reviews are good but the publisher doesn't buy the next one. And we do this *again and again*—on deadline no less!—like total jackasses. We're Paul Atreides sticking his hand in the Reverend Mother's creepy pain box, except then we go back for seconds, thirds, tenths, again and again like utter masochists.[6]

Holy crap, sometimes a single bad review will derail our day. On the one hand, it doesn't even make sense—you think, "I just got ten great reviews, and here's one bad one, shouldn't that still feel good? If this were a grade school test I'd still be rocking an A, so isn't that great?" But also, it makes a bit more sense when you contextualize it as, "I just ate a delicious seven-course dinner, every bite a shining gem, and then in the final course, I found rat poops in the butterscotch *pot de crème*."[7] I guarantee you those poops have ruined the *entire meal*.

It's not just us getting rejected by one person—we're putting

---

6   "What's in the box?" "*Pain*." "Oh, okay, lemme try again, maybe next time it'll be candy."

7   Or should I say, *Poo de crème* . . . I'm so sorry, it was right there, I can't help myself.

a book out in front of hundreds, thousands, even more. We are *destined* for heartbreak. And honestly, even before you get to that point, the job is pretty weird. As noted elsewhere, it can feel pretty lonely, pretty isolating. You're crawling through the dark forest of your writing day in and day out, absolutely un-sure how you're doing, or if this trash you're collecting on the page will ever be recycled into something beautiful, or if it will forever remain just a landfill of rotten nouns and fetid verbs. It has the vibe of a sensory deprivation tank, except you're not physically depriving yourself of sense—no, this one is intellec-tual, emotional. Living with your writing for a long period of time is, in a way, also living with yourself for a long period of time. And that can be *really fucked up.*

Which is where it becomes important for us to counterbal-ance all of this by venting pressure, by rewarding ourselves, by caring about what we do even when others don't. It's up to us to apply self-care.

Let's play it out, find more specifics, and examine the ques-tions of:

How do I take care of myself and my work?

How do I bring kindness into my own writing life?

The Space-Time Continuum

You are going to meet many people in your life who will not take your writing seriously. I wish this weren't so. Sometimes the people who won't take it seriously will be some of the most important people in your life—friends, loved ones, coworkers. Maybe they don't even think they're *not* taking it seriously. Maybe they just don't see it. But many really will disregard the

It is up to you to ensure that you still treat the writing like the real thing it is.

seriousness of this thing, and so it is up to you to ensure that you still treat the writing like the real thing it is.

First, this means carving out time to do the thing. If you want to write, you must set aside time to write. This doesn't need to be every day, and it doesn't need to be for hours on end, but just by securing some proper time for yourself, it helps tell you and everyone else in your life, *Hey, this is important to me.*

It also means finding the *space* to do it. Everyone has a different process in terms of where they like to write or, moreover, where they can and cannot write. That whole clichéd "writer writing in a coffee shop" thing? Yeah, I can't do that. Can't now, couldn't then. If ever you saw me in a coffee shop writing, then you saw someone who wanted to perform writing instead of actually writing. Now I have friends who love to write in public spaces, which is great. It works for them, and they know this, and that's the ideal. I generally had to find somewhere quiet—hell, in one job there was a closet I ducked into in order to bang out some fast words. And eventually it became essential to have an office in the house, however small, to write in—and, these days, I actually write in the ~~Murder~~ Writing Shed in my backyard.[8] The reason behind retrofitting the shed into a writing

---

8   It's a shed that used to house lawnmowers and snow shovels and a liberal dose of mice. But it's now a cool space with a bookshelf and my computer and a couch and split-system HVAC so okay it's not *exactly* just a shed anymore, but it was, once. It got a glow-up. Also an oubliette where I keep my critics. Ha ha just kidding. Probably. Hey, could you stand a few more inches to your left? Thanks.

space was because, as my kiddo got a little older—I think this was when he was four or five years old—he pretty much lost all semblance of understanding boundaries. I could close my office door and he would come flying in, HELLO DADDY I WOULD LIKE TO PLAY STAR WARS NOW, and I mean holy shit I'm not a *monster*, of course I would play Star Wars with him. Ironically, at this time I also had an *actual* Star Wars book to write, and playing Star Wars with a four-year-old turns out is not actually equivalent to writing said Star Wars book.[9]

Here you might say, "Well, you could've just locked him out," and I did, but those with young children understand that every day with a kid is like the scene in *Jurassic Park* where the velociraptors learn to open doors. My son would find his way into the office somehow. I'd see fingers wiggling under the door like he was a zombie. That kid would John McClane his way in through the ducts.

An external office became essential, so that's what I did.

Taking the work seriously doesn't need to be that extravagant (or privileged)—it was only that way for me after years of being a professional writer. But even before that, I tried to secure time and place for the work. I tried to make sure I made time for reading and education. I also made sure I surrounded myself with others who also took it seriously and who respected

---

9   I note here too that in writing the first *Star Wars: Aftermath* book, I was given three months to write the first draft. Which is not a lot of time. But then suddenly they moved up the publication date from November that year to September, which, if you can do simple math, is two months sooner. Which meant they also needed the book . . . you guessed it, two months sooner. Three months minus two months equals, yup, one month. I had *one month* to write the first draft of that book. And I goddamn jolly well fucking did it, too. And building the Writing Shed was an essential part of that.

my time and my writing and the work that goes into it.[10]
Find people who respect your time and your desires. That
is perhaps the greatest kindness of
them all.

*Find people
who respect
your time and
your desires.*

Well, that and getting paid for your
writing. Specifically, getting paid an
equitable amount. Which, admittedly,
is on a pretty wide sliding scale, but
that is another way to take yourself se-
riously: demand recompense for the work when it is essential
to do so. The work is worth something. Make sure you make a
claim on that worth. Don't get taken for a ride. Don't give the
work away for free unless it's part of a smart strategy to do
so—remember, you cannot pay rent or buy groceries with exposure. Hikers die from exposure, and so can artists.

Harlan Ellison wisely demanded people *pay the writers*, and
that's as true now as it was then. Get paid if that's where you're
at in your writing life. Get paid, because the work is hard, and
you deserve it.[11]

---

10   Hell, even at this point in my career I still have people who are like,
"Can you do these *other non-writing things* during the day?" as if my writing
job is just me lying in the soft lawn grass. I remind those people I am at
work during the day, even if I work from home, and then I drop them into
the shed oubliette, which as I told you is definitely not real ha ha shut up.

11   It probably demands special note here that not every writer is in this
thing because they want to sell the work, and I support that. And not every
story is going to earn you money—I only mean to say that, if someone is
going to publish it, then taking the work seriously means getting paid for
that and not simply handing it over, for free. But it's also okay, if you're in
control of the work, to give it out freely. Don't be exposed, but rather, *expose
yourself.* Uhh. You know what I mean.

Human Kindling

Self-care is also looking for the warning lights on the dashboard lighting up. You know the one that says something vague like CHECK ENGINE? Yeah, well, we writers have a check engine light. And mine is warning me about one thing:

Burnout.

Burnout is real.

I didn't really know it was a thing for a long time, or at least I assumed it was something that happened to *other* people.

And then it happened to me, so now I keep an eye out for it. In case it comes sneaking up on me—because honestly, it always seems to sneak, and doesn't like to announce its presence.

What is burnout, exactly?

For me, and it may be different for you, it feels like exhaustion. It's not writer's block, exactly, as usually I still have the ideas, I just feel like getting those ideas out onto the page is a fight. I feel like I'm losing the throughline. I feel fatigued by the very idea of writing. Now this can also be depression, but for me, the line between the two is that burnout comes as a clear consequence of pushing too hard: too many assignments, too many words to write, too many deadlines, whatever. You push and push and push and eventually it feels a bit like trying to do karate in a mud-pit. It's emptying. Exhausting.

It's twee-sounding, but it feels a whole lot like, *I really need a vacation from this.* Not a permanent one. But a break that brings a breath of fresh air.

To deviate for a moment—

I had a doctor who one time compared allergies to having a

cup, suggesting that it's not always that we are immediately allergic to a thing; sometimes it's about allergens overall filling up that cup, and when the cup is overfull, the spillover is our allergic reaction. Is this true? I have no idea. But I find that it's a pretty good metaphor for various neurodivergences and also for the act of writing itself. Look at it this way: everyone has a cup. That cup is differently sized for everybody, but one thing is true universally: it has a finite volume in which to pour stress. And if your writing life is filling up that cup too much, too fast, the spillover might look a lot like burnout. Or, if you are a sufferer of those maladies, it might lend itself to depression or anxiety. Protect the cup and know when you're overfilling it.

Having run up against burnout, I now try to moderate my life in an effort to prevent it from happening in the first place—meaning, I try to not overfill the cup. I take breaks—usually I write for forty-five minutes, then take fifteen minutes to, well, not write. I don't pile on contracts and try to write only one or two books a year instead of the three or four I was writing. I try not to push, too. If I write during my allotted time or hit my word count, I'll continue on if I'm feeling it—but I don't break myself if not. People want a lot from me and, I think, from most writers, and I also think there's this deep urge for us to pay it back and pay it forward. Which is a good urge! You should. I try to. But there's also value in recognizing when people want to take more than you have to give. Because that *also* leads to burnout. We are each a deep, strange forest. Do not set it on fire for warmth and for light. Because soon?

All you'll be is ashes.

Indiana Jones and the Temple of Meat

I operate on the theory that the writing comes from my mind, but my mind is housed in this floppy, gloppy meat-soup skin-sack that is called my "body," so the best thing I can do for my writing is to keep this meat-soup skin-sack in the best working order. That's not to say I am in some kind of *peak physical condition*. I only mean that I try not to run my body through the garbage disposal of human existence. It may not be a temple, as noted, but I'm also not going to treat it like a New Jersey rest stop.

Here is what works for me: I try to eat protein during the day, not carbs, unless it's fruit. I also operate on a regular schedule. And finally, I care very much about ergonomics. Both standing all day and sitting all day are hell on your body,[12] though really only if you're not caring for your posture and your musculoskel-etal[13] needs. I know "lumbar support" is not the sexiest phrase in the human language, but it's definitely sexier than "I threw my back out just because I sat wrong for four hours and now I need you to help me get off the toilet because all my vertebrae have locked up tighter than a Disney nondisclosure agreement."

To recap: I try to eat well. I rely on ergonomics. I walk, I run,

---

12 I assume the natural position of humans is "supine."

13 As I was typing it, I was like, "This isn't really a word, is it? It doesn't sound like a real word." I said it out loud a bunch of times. MUS CYOO LO SKELL UH TULL. It sounds like nonsense. But then I googled it and it's totally real. Because all of language is nonsense! It's all just gibbering mouth noises that we all loosely agree mean something. Some words mean one thing and somehow also mean their own opposite! Which doesn't sound possible, but here we are. What fun!

I do strength-training exercises in the shed. I meditate. I fight bears.[14]

Care for the container of meat-soup you call a human body. Your writing needs it.

Treat Yo Self

Of course, I still reward myself. Like a dog, I respond very, very well to food rewards. Don't get me wrong! I'll take praise and petting, too. But fuck yeah, *treats*. Tacos. Ice cream. Fancy chocolates. Oh my god, give me a weird gourmet donut? Hnnnngh. Yes. Hell yes. It's just, as with all things, I try to moderate this. I don't write a paragraph and cheer for myself while powering through a pint of ice cream. "I did it! I finished a chapter! Time to eat a whole damn cheesecake and drink this entire gallon of white wine!" I don't want to destroy myself with treats. It's not even an every-day thing. If I finish a full draft, I'll get some Jeni's ice cream or something.

Care for the container of meat-soup you call a human body.

But rewards don't always have to be purely bound to baser pleasures. Those are good! I like those. But it's also good to treat your brain in different ways. More *creative* ways.

---

14   Sorry, to clarify, I fight bears in my mind, while meditating. Thinking of punching an angry grizzly bear is soothing to me. I would never fight a bear in real life because I love animals too much, but definitely not because a bear would maul me into blood pudding. That's not it at all. How dare you slander me in such a way. What are you, a bear?

Have Something Creative That Is Not Writing

Something that has nothing to do with money or output or anything.

For me, it's photography. I really have no skills in that department—sure, I have a rudimentary understanding of shutter speed and f-stop and ISO and all that, but I'm not super dialed into it, and I really don't want to be. Mostly, I have a camera. I have some lenses. I go out into the world and I take hundreds, if not thousands, of digital photos, only a fraction of which are worth a damn. I do this because it is relaxing. Because I like to hang out with bugs and birds.[15] I take pictures of flowers and leaves. It's nice. It gets me out of my head. I don't even think about my story all that much. It is a vital escape hatch and not doing it in a professional capacity ensures that it is all for the fun of it and has none of the pressures that accompany the things we do for a living.[16]

You, of course, can do differently.

It doesn't even have to be that creative. Just something that's an outlet for you that takes you away from the writing but also flexes different skills, talents, and intellectual muscles. Engine repair, board games, painting D&D miniatures, following along with Bob Ross and his happy little trees, playing the drums, cooking, baking, assassinations, heirloom apple reviewing, bear-fighting, possum-collecting, graphic design, game

---

15 Fuck yeah, nature.

16 I note here that I have sold a few photographs in my time, which I think technically makes me a "professional photographer," but I sold those entirely by accident, so I don't think it counts.

design, demon summoning, coffee roasting, oubliette architecture, Jazzercise, amateur bioterrorism, knitting, pottery,

Have   contemplating the universe on yard
                          mushrooms, etc.
something   I'd only suggest ensuring that
                          whatever outlet and expression you
creative that   choose, it is one that is not in any way
is not writing.   adjacent to writing. Reading doesn't

count—you should be doing that anyway. Screenwriting, poetry, whatever, they're all still *writing*, so maybe it's not quite a
perfect outlet.

Though as with all things, you do you.

Protect Yourself by Literally Protecting Your Writing

Here's a form of self-care you're not thinking about:

Back up your writing.

Back. Up. Your. Writing.

BACK UP YOUR WRITING.

Insert a thousand exclamation points here.

Those who possess penises tend to zip themselves up in a
pants zipper *one time ever*, and after that, you remain ever-
vigilant not to do it again. And so it is the same for those who
have lost huge chunks of writing—if not an entire draft—from
not properly backing up your stuff.

So let me get ahead of this and remind you:

Do it. Do it often. Do it completely. Losing that work is a
sharp knife to the gut and it is key to be protective of the work
and your own soul on this.

Here is what I do:

I back up the draft to Dropbox, never backing it up to the same file twice.

I back it up to an external hard drive.

I also email it to myself.

Three separate backups.

I also have my computer plugged into a UPS battery backup power brick, so that means even loss of electricity doesn't automatically cause my computer to power down, thus losing the thing I'm working on. It gives me time to save the work and not just watch it blink into the void.

Some of Your Tools May Be Broken

And now, we speak of a forbidden subject:

HAM.

Wait, that can't be right.

Hold on, let me check my notes.

Ah, haha, sorry, the paper got folded up a little bit. Missed some letters. Let's just unfold this sucker like an origami cootie-catcher and . . .

Now we speak of the forbidden subject:

SHAME.

Once upon a time, I felt that shame was an essential tool in my toolbox. Self-shame, to be clear, not necessarily the shaming of others. I've wanted to be a writer since a very early age, and so when I did not achieve some aspect of that goal— whether we're talking about how I didn't finish a story, or wrote a story I wasn't happy with, or whatever—I felt shame. More to the point, I *chose* to feel shame. I don't know that this choice was particularly a conscious one, but I do think it was a thing that I unconsciously chose. I opened the door. I let it in.

We are taught to feel shame.

I did this because it's often how we're made to feel when we fail in some way. If we do something not up to standard, if we do not complete a task, we experience shame. We feel that shame because we are taught to feel shame. This country that we live in is ultimately a very sort of . . . puritanical, prosperity-gospel, carceral-state, it's-all-your-fault-if-something-bad-happens country. Right? And I'm not trying to absolve anybody of responsibility for themselves or their actions, but we ultimately oversimplify this shaming to the point of punitive absurdity. Anything we fail at is because, in some distant way, we believe we have sinned and deserve it. Our failures are entirely our own and can in no way be tied to outside forces.

And let's say that's even true! Sometimes we do fail and it's because we own that failure, snout to tail, brow to butthole. Is that really a sin? Or is failure, as discussed elsewhere, an opportunity to grow? To do differently?

Problem is, I, like many others, assumed it was a sin (in the non-religious sense). We beat ourselves up for our failures and indiscretions, and we feel like that's a productive way to get better. It's the *hot stove* approach—touch a hot stove once, you'll never touch it again. But that's not what shame is. Shame isn't just touching the hot stove, experiencing the pain of that poor choice, and learning from it. Shame is feeling bad *in addition* to feeling bad. It's guilt. It's self-hatred. Failure and rejection already feel bad. We don't need to add layers of misery on top of it, like slathering spider icing upon a cake made of live scorpions. Touching the hot stove is punishment enough. But we feel bad *for* touching the hot stove, which is *in addition* to the pain of touching the hot stove.

We flagellate ourselves over our failures, and in that flagellation, all we learn is that failure is pain. It's not an opportunity. It's not a chance to learn and do better. It's just an opportunity to suffer, and so avoiding failure at all costs becomes paramount, because we don't want to feel that way again. Problem, though: failure is baked into this thing we do. Hell, it's baked into everything. Failure is a default state, and it is a necessary one. But if all we feel is shame over it, and all we want to do is avoid it—then we're likelier to lock up, to refuse to begin something because beginning something means failing at something. We're less likely to take the kinds of chances that are essential to our *success*. We get so twisted up, so bound in knots, we can't move, can't make, can't do anything except live in fear. It's why you praise a dog instead of punishing it. Punishment just makes the poor thing scared and anxious. Praise, however, ingrains good behaviors and routines. And self-care performs that function, too.

> *Failure is baked into this thing we do.*

Which means self-care involves accepting that shame is not part of your self-care regimen. Feeling bad about not finishing a story or getting a bad review isn't going to fix it. Some things can't be fixed, and those that can are only fixed by fixing them. If you break your arm, feeling guilty about it doesn't heal the arm. And it doesn't even help you not break the arm next time—the most it does is make you averse to all risk instead of taking smart risks.

Shame is half-a-ladder. It feels like it's progress, like you're climbing it, like you're using it to reach greater heights—but it only gets you part of the way there. The rest of the ladder is missing. The next level remains out of reach.

Avoid shame. Don't include it as part of your routine.

=

YOU CAN ALSO avoid shame that comes from others.

By which I mean you need to avoid your bad reviews.

Mostly. Usually. I'll clarify.

I have been tagged in my fair share of bad reviews of my books across social media, and when said bad reviewer is confronted by someone saying, "Hey, you don't need to tag the author in your bad review," this bad reviewer usually says something like, BUT HOW WILL THEY LEARN, THEY NEED TO FIX IT, as if they're giving you *pure golden wisdom* here, and you're just too butt-stung to see it. They seem to feel that their criticism exists solely as a corrective and not, for instance, a subjective pop-culture opinion that is, at best, helping guide other readers, and at worst, a toxic bleat into the void.

When I was first starting out as a writer, I would read every bad review I could find. Because I felt the same way, that somehow I could read all these reviews and use them as a collective corrective—and there is perhaps something to that, for if every review of your work calls out something about it, maybe that something is a thing you need to at least consider, if not address.

Just the same, it's important to realize that not every review or criticism is created equal. There's a difference in reading a review from *The New York Times* or *Kirkus* and reading some angry screed from @HitlerTickles6969 on Twitter, y'know? One assumes the latter is not exactly well trained in literary criticism. Honestly, even professional reviewers aren't necessarily trained that way. I've had books reviewed across the breadth and depth of professional outlets, and while I don't know that I've had any real *stinker* reviews, you get some mixed-bag reviews tucked in there. And looking back now, I'm not sure that devotedly reading all the random negative reviews on Amazon or Goodreads was that useful. I can't say that I've really changed how I write based on bad reviews. At this point I'm usually more interested in what I hear from my agent or from my editors.

You don't need to be a giant open doorway for anybody to walk through.

I don't know that you need to cloister yourself away from all bad reviews, but I also don't know that they're particularly valuable. And so it goes that part of self-care as a writer is about understanding and limiting the access to yourself. What I mean is, you don't need to be a giant open doorway for anybody to walk through. Once, publishers used to very explicitly ask for writers to have a "platform" on social media—a place to interface with readers and to "put themselves out there"—but I've seen a lot of publishers pull back on that, seeing how fraught that path really is. Which means . . .

We Need to Talk About the Internet

Writers need the internet.

Everybody does, really. It's a vital resource—once a fringe digital luxury, the internet is now one of the most important aspects of our daily lives. Ordering goods, applying for jobs, wasting endless hours looking at dog pictures. And for writers, oof, c'mon, how do you avoid it? Research. Communication. Outreach to agents and editors. Water-cooler chat with other writers and publishing professionals. Emails. So many emails. Too many emails.[17] And did I mention the dog photos??

And then there's social media.

For me, my ~~drug~~ social media outlet of choice is Twitter.[18]

Depending on whom you talk to, I am either a Cautionary Tale of Twitter or a Raging Twitter Success story. Reality is, it's both.

On Twitter I've:

- Met some of my most favoritest people and have truly earned some wonderful friendships.

- Met some of the worst humanity has to offer and earned some trolls and stalkers who harass me to this very day.

- Gone viral, and as a result, had books published[19] and a movie made.[20]

- Gone viral and been besieged by sewer clowns for increments of time equal to hours, days, weeks, months, even *years.*

- Been lauded, cheered, feted, hurrahed.

---

17 JESUS GOD THE EMAILS.

18 I would do TikTok, but I'm already considered cringe online. Nobody needs to see me galumphing about, pointing at things or snapping my fingers, dancing for you so you'll buy my books.

19 *You Can Do Anything, Magic Skeleton.*

20 *You Might Be the Killer.*

- Been bullied, impersonated, threatened with death and rape, doxed.

- Got my Star Wars writing gig just by tweeting about it.

- Lost my Star Wars writing gig years later because alt-right sewer clowns and their bot-armies mobbed me up.[21]

- Had some of my best days.

- Had some of my very worst days.

And that's not to mention the sheer weight of mis/disinformation about me—just an endless stream of people assuring themselves and one another that I am literally the worst person on Earth for a reason that isn't even close to true. And that's just me, a straight white cisgender able-bodied dude. I've seen women and POC get ten times the hate. The question becomes, Is the juice worth the squeeze?

Being on social media is having access to everyone on there. And you're also giving *them* access to *you*.

Which . . . can be fraught. You're inviting thousands upon thousands of strangers not just into your house, but into your *head* and your *heart*.

Publishers used to expect you to be on there, but that value proposition seems to have changed, as being on there also means you're now exposed not just to readers and fans and

---

21 Aja Romano, "The New Troll: How Bots and Puppets Make Internet Outrage Seem Louder Than It Is," *Vox*, October 24, 2018, https://www.vox.com/culture/2018/10/24/17995502/twitter-trolls-bots-chuck-wendig-bethany-lacina.

other writers, but also to some of the most toxic, abusive people on the planet.[22] There was once this sense that you could
get on there and sell books, but that was perhaps never really
true[23]—and these days any books you do sell come with a cost
possibly greater than we'd care to admit, a cost to your mental
and emotional health.

When I first started using Twitter, I found it to be a useful
watercooler space for the lonely life of being a writer. It put you
in touch with other writers, publishing professionals, and,
widening the circle, other awesome humans—artists and di-
rectors and poets and so forth. And it's why I always thought
that while Twitter was not amazing for hand-selling your
books, it *was* a wonderful place to connect with other storytellers and such. It still had that professional value—but it was
about making those connections instead of pushing a single
book sale. And not making connections in a way of seeing
other humans as just a resource, as favors to be gotten, but as
people who genuinely understood you and whom you understood in turn. Acquaintances and friends.

And then, somewhere along the way, Twitter stopped
becoming a watercooler and it became a stage. Except all the
audience was up on stage with you. Everybody was perform-
ing, 24/7, whether they wanted to be or not.

And *then*, maybe around 2016, it stopped being a stage.

It became a fight club.

And whether it's your first night or your five hundredth—

---

22 Not to mention, their endless sock puppets, bots, and whatever rogue
artificial intelligences have claimed the space.

23 To clarify, you can definitely sell tens or even hundreds of copies of
books via Twitter, but publishers need you to sell thousands to break even.

You have to fight.

At least, that's how it feels. It's a tough place where you never really know if you're engaging with something real, someone true, or if you're part of disinformation . . . or someone's revenge . . . or injustice cloaked in the raiment of justice. It gets really hard to tell up from down. Further, it's a chute lubed slick with sheer, liquid doom. You can fall into that social media pit very, very easily and just . . . sit there and flick through page after page, growing more anxious, growing more upset, wanting to start throwing punches and gnashing your teeth.

Meanwhile, you're not writing at all.

That paints social media in a particularly negative light—and I don't know that it's entirely fair, either. But it's a rough place and has gotten worse, I think, and I can say as a writer I know it can be very easy to not only become distracted by it, but also be dragged down by it. All the things that make you popular on Twitter are also the things that make you a target on Twitter. A larger presence and platform on that place also means more arrows shot in your back.

That's not easy. And it's not really a kindness to yourself.

So self-care sometimes means limiting people's access to you. Strangers, especially. It's okay to lock down your social media. It's perfectly fine to limit your usage of it. You do not need to engage with it full-throatedly every day. Use it to seek joy and friends and information, and if it's not giving you those things, if all it feels like is you gargling sewage from an endlessly regurgitating pipe, then maybe it's time to step away. It's not meant to be some kind of gauntlet you have to run. You don't need to give it your

Self-care sometimes means limiting people's access to you.

attention, or everyone else the access. You can be free, whether that means moderating your presence there or just getting all the way out. If you find it stressing you out or distracting you too much? Take a break, be it temporary or permanent. It's okay. We all need it.

The Long View

Obviously, there are lots of other little things you can do—

Oh, get a massage! Get enough sleep![24] Spend time with friends and family! Keep a reflective journal! Maintain a vigorous, constantly updated enemies list!

But it's not just about picking and choosing one thing over another. It's not about, "Oh, have a Reese's peanut butter cup after a tough edit!"[25] It's more about viewing yourself holistically and trying to create good habits—habits that reward and protect you, and by proxy, that protect your writing as well.

I think the overall message here is:

Writing is hard.

The writing life is also hard.

So go easy on yourself. Reality will get in plenty of kicks and punches. There's no reason to add to them. Be kind to yourself and your writing, because there's really no guarantee that anyone else will be.

---

24   In this economy?!

25   Though also that sounds pretty good right now. I'm going to go eat a peanut butter cup. Hold tight.

Something Important, Part Two

A BREAK IN THE FLOW TO SAY:
Some days, you rescue the writing.
Other days, the writing rescues you.

6

The Danger of the Myth of the Starving Artist

A ROMANTIC NOTION PERSISTS: THE ARTIST, THE writer, crammed in a tiny city apartment, water stains above their head, mice running in the wall. But they are bent over a beautiful creation: a painting, a story, a dish on a menu, a clay figurine. They have flowers next to them, not in a vase, but in a Snapple bottle. The window is open, and the night is starry and warm, and the sounds of the city provide the eternal soundtrack. Though the writer wears thrift store finds, they're stylish enough, retro in a way. A bowl of ramen sits nearby, already cooling because, being so consumed by the process of creation, the artist has forgotten to eat. Because the art is everything. This is the artist's chance. They are choosing to be a maker, a creator, someone who *Does the Thing*, and they have no job, they have no prospects but for this half-made art in front of them. They have chosen to jump out of the plane without a parachute, dangerously, madly, *wonderfully* assured that they will figure out how to make a parachute on the way down.

Follow your dreams, writers.

Reckless abandon.

Give your art your everything.

Tell your story at any cost.

It all sounds quite nice.

It's not that this is entirely wrong—I do think a life in service to art and story is one that features a little bit of sacrifice, at least in the sense that when you choose to do something it means you perhaps close other doors. Eventually, picking a path means rejecting other paths. You can go back and return to those rejected paths, but that requires different sacrifices, including the sacrifice of time and effort. As the idea goes, we only have so much time in our day, and so many days in our life, and so get busy writing, or that time is lost.

> *A life in service to art and story is one that features a little bit of sacrifice.*

But there's a line.

A very important line.

It is one thing to take your work seriously and give it your all. It is another where you sacrifice a normal life and its essentials in its pursuit.

To cut to the chase here:

You shouldn't be ashamed of having a day job.

Cash Registers, Crashed Vans, and How Day Jobs Help Make the Words Go

I wanted to be a writer since I was pretty young. It was eighth grade when I realized, "Oh, holy shit, you can do this for a living?" It's not like I thought books grew on trees or were written just for the magnanimity of having written one—"I just love bringing joy with the written word! I need no recompense, for your readership is reward *enough!*"—I just hadn't really sussed out that it was a viable career path. Once I realized that, it was like a revelation. And with that revelation, I was off to the races.

Went to college. Got a degree.

Right out of college, I knew: *I'm going to be a writer, so I should take a writing job.* I found a writing job writing for the ICRDA, which is a fancy acronym that stands for, oh hold on because it's about to get really exciting up in here:

The

International

Cash

Register

Dealers

Association.

The ICRDA.

It is, quite literally, an organization that's devoted *not* to *making* cash registers or POS[1] devices, but rather, to the *distribution* and *sales* of them.

And this organization had a—drum roll, please—*newspaper.*

YEAH, PARTY TIME, BABY. PANTS-OFF DANCE-OFF AT THE CASH REGISTER ASSOCIATION, IT'S GETTING ALL INTERNATIONAL UP IN HERE, WOOOOO.

Ahem.

So.

I applied. I got the job. And my first job out of school was as a writer for a newspaper devoted to the sales *of* point-of-sale devices. It was as thrilling as it sounds, which is to say, it was

---

1   Point-of-sale, not, er, the other thing.

like watching turtles fuck.[2] Or, it would have been that thrilling if I was even writing that much, which I was not. They
hired me and I did very little writing and a whole lot of, like,
moving boxes and filing papers and making copies. The idea
being, I guess, blah blah blah, everybody's gotta chip in, right?
Ground floor means you do some ground floor work. At least I
could call myself a writer? Or something?

At one point, though, one of the sales guys stopped me in
the hallway. This was not a guy I liked very much—the first
person you picture when I say "corporate sales guy from the
late '90s?" Yeah, that's him. Which is to say, bad cologne, cheap
suit, big attitude, jokes that weren't jokes so much as they were
jabs at the expense of everyone around him. But he did me a
favor that day. He said, "You know, we don't like to hire temps
around here." Blink, blink. "Okay," I said, not sure what he was
getting at.

Sales Guy explained.

"See, temps from temp agencies, they aren't committed to
the work that much. They know the job is—it's right there in
the name, *temporary*. So what this company likes to do is
hire full-timers for bullshit temp work. They give them a title
that doesn't really apply, and then that employee just does
grunt work."

I was probably slower on the uptake than I'd like to admit,
but before too long I was picking up what he was laying down.
He didn't even have to wink at me salaciously in order to drive
the point home.

I was a writer.

Sorry, a "writer."

---

2   In slow-motion.

But really, I was a temp worker. An office monkey. A box-hauler.

Now, to be clear, there's no shame in any of that work—but there is a whole lot of shame for a company not willing to be clear to its employees about what they're there to do. I wasn't really doing the job I was hired to do. They dangled the bait. I took the bait. I wasn't a professional writer at all.

Of course, I still needed money, so I kept the job for a while, with an eye on the exit door. And as a postscript, that exit door came not long after—

Once more, treating me like the non-writer I actually was, the boss above my boss[3] had a new task for me. They were having some kind of annual conference hootenanny, and they wanted *me* to drive a tour van around and give some of the Cash Register Fancypantses a tour of the city. This city being Charlotte, North Carolina, a city that had only been my home for a little over four years at that point, not a city I was comfortable giving a tour of, but they said it'd be fine and I was to do this task. *All right, I'll just make some stuff up,* I decided, embracing the idea that this was part of my job as a writer—to tell a glorious fiction. "That's the Bank of America building," I might say, "and fun fact, it's shaped like that because it is an antenna to the Capitalist Hell God, Blubb-Shorrggorth, The Lord of Bloodied Coin."

They gave me keys and directed me to the van, which was in a parking garage nearby.

Except, it wasn't really a van.

It was more like a minibus. It was fucking huge. I don't

---

3   My boss was actually very nice and may not have known I was a rented chimp.

know if I needed a special license to drive it, but it sure *felt* like
I did. Either way, I thought, *Well, I'm in too deep now*—so I
started it up and headed toward the exit.

Funny thing, though. I did not realize that oversized vehi-
cles have their own special exit. Nobody told me this. I just
assumed I could go out the usual way, so I headed to the
usual exit, not really realizing that the aperture of escape
was, uhh . . .

A little too tight.

I suddenly discovered that the "van" was vibrating, and
then came the sound of grinding metal out the driver's window as the side of the minibus scraped along the ticket-reader
machine that granted egress. I thought, perhaps foolishly,
"Well, the only way out is through," so I gently pressed the accelerator, hoping that the situation was not too bad.

The metal-on-metal sound increased.

The vehicle slowed and then stopped.

Even with me trying to accelerate.

I had lodged the goddamn thing in the exit like cholesterol
in an artery.

It was the one exit, too. And other cars were starting to
drive in behind me.

I gave it a moment, and then I decided, *Welp, that's my
cue*, and I took out the keys, sat them on the driver's seat,
climbed out the passenger-side window, and left. I found a pay
phone,[4] called my boss, told her what had happened, and then
said, "You probably should've hired a real tour guide. Anyway!
I quit."

And then I walked to my car and drove home.

---

4   This was in the ANTEDILUVIAN days where cell phones did not exist.

(It was a little like walking away from an explosion, and it felt kinda rad.)

Anyway! From there I had the classic random slapdash spate of jobs so common to writers: I sold Gateway computers, I slung coffee, I worked at Borders bookstore thinking they were hiring me to sell books but actually it was just to sling more coffee. I moved back to Pennsylvania, where my father got me a job at his company. He wouldn't tell me what I was doing. First day of the job, he walked me through a labyrinth of pigment plants and warehouses until we ended up at the far end of the complex in an abandoned warehouse where a literal pyramid of filthy file boxes waited, piled so high it was easily twice my height. And then he wheeled out an industrial paper shredder that they called "The Bitch,"[5] whereupon he explained that my job was to take down each file box, open it up, pull out the files inside, and shred them. The shredder could take a file thick as my fist and just *grrrmmrrggrwwwggghvvbbbbt* chew it to fucking bits in one go. You could lose a hand to this. So this was my task. All day. Eight hours. Stand there, shred documents— and when I asked what the documents were, I was told they were documents the company did not want the EPA to see, so ha ha, I was probably doing something illegal? It's fine. Everything was fine!

At the end of the day, having done little else, I was covered head to toe in black dust. Like soot. Maybe it was pigment. My spit was ink-dark. I was coughing up sooty sputum. It was nasty business.

---

5   I apologize for the word, but I felt it necessary to cleave to the truth of this story. It is what they called the device.

On the way home I knew, well, I can't go back there tomorrow.

So, on a lark, I stopped in a shopping center, determined to find a job, any job, so help me Jesus. And there, a new bargain-basement bookstore had opened up. I walked in and met the manager, a Greek guy named Pete.

Pete hired me on the spot as the assistant manager.

So then I started a job at this bookstore, whereupon my manager, Pete, would regale me with tales from when he ran a bar in Philly. One day he lifted up his shirt and showed me a series of bullet hole scars. He said someone shot up the bar he was in and he got shot a bunch of times, and he told me this like it was just Another Day in the Life of Pete. Pete also would do this thing where he handed me an empty cardboard box and would say, "Go fill this with books, then go put them in your trunk." He knew I liked reading and writing and wanted to help me, so he uhhh let me just take the books? Again, probably illegal, much like crashing a van or shredding EPA documents. I might be a criminal. I shouldn't be writing this all down. Ha ha it's all a joke none of this happened![6] Regardless, it's how I read all the Gaiman Sandman books and got cool books about angels and demons and mythology. Hell, I still have a bunch of books from those occasional free-for-all book hauls.

I eventually did other things, too. I was an IT manager for a necktie merchandising company. I did web design (despite having no training in web design) for a post-payola-but-still-payola radio-play website. I did temp work out the wazoo. I worked for the local library both as marketing outreach to

6   The Aristocrats!

underserved communities and as an assistant to the teen librarians and book-buyers. I helped a man named Tom Nook develop an island resort, and also he may not have been a man but some kind of capitalist raccoon-monster forcing me to mine Bitcoin in the middle of the ocean?[7]

And here, reading this, you might be thinking, "Well, this all sounds moderately stupid and occasionally terrible. How is this encouraging again? Why are day jobs a good thing?"

Well, let me tell you.

First, because *I was not starving and I had a roof over my head*. Turns out, those two things are really, really huge components to actually trying to be a writer. When I didn't have a job? When I was scraping together pennies and selling plasma for coin, do you think I was at my most productive? Spoiler warning: I was not. Starvation is not a good condition for making art. Being worried about where your next paycheck is going to come from does not make it easy to effortlessly create art. Half the time I'd want to spend writing I'd instead spend just looking for jobs. It was easier to write when I was working jobs, despite jobs taking up the lion's share of time.

Starvation is not a good condition for making art.

And, on the flip side of it, having those moderately stupid and occasionally terrible jobs also reminded me that this was not what I wanted to do for a living. So it gave the impetus to push, to look for different, to look for better, and to keep on writing every moment I could spare. Before work, during lunch breaks, after work, I'd write. And eventually I seized an

---

7   This *might've* been a video game. Things blur.

opportunity to write freelance for pen-and-paper game companies and did that for just over a decade.

But I *still* didn't quit my day job for years into that freelance gig.

When I did, it was a difficult transition: I had to learn to budget, to really chase deadlines, to chase jobs. And when I transitioned from freelance to writing novels, that was tough, too—that first year was a dry well in terms of income.

(A brief story within the story here, too: The reason I took the library job mentioned earlier was because though I was turning a reasonable income as a freelancer, trying to get a mortgage for our first house was a nonstarter. The bank simply had no idea what a freelancer or "independent contractor" even was. They treated me like I was some kind of unicorn, except the bad version of a unicorn.[8] They just kept wanting to know who my boss was, what company employed me. So to get a mortgage, I needed the kind of job that offered a steady paycheck.)

And getting to go full-time as a writer was, for me, an epic and profound privilege. I only got to do it in part because the freelance work became so much that I had to either cut *it* or the day job out. I couldn't continue to do both. And even then, that privilege was born of being married to someone who had a job that offered us pretty cherry health insurance.[9] Because seri-

---

8   A pee-yewnicorn.

9   Eventually, when she left her job to raise our son, I was doing pretty well as a novelist—and we could afford health insurance only because of the ACA's health insurance marketplace and subsidies. Just in case you feel like being mad at "Obamacare" any time soon—despite its imperfections, the ACA is literally partly responsible for you reading this book right now. And let me also say that health care—not just insurance—should be available to

ously, just like you need food to live and a roof over your head? You need the security of health care. Setting aside the fact that health *insurance* is not the same as health *care*, it's what we have in this country, and it gets a whole lot harder to write if you're underwater from medical bills or medical conditions. Health care is key. Which means—

There is zero shame in a day job. Part-time, full-time, whatever. And a day job may very well be crucial, because writing—as a hobby, as a semi-pro endeavor, or as a fully professional gig—is not always a delivery system for reliable income. Hell, even when the money is good, it can arrive erratically. Feast or famine. During times of famine, a day job will keep you fed.

There is zero shame in a day job.

Most artists have day jobs.

That's how it works. Because the alternative is often starvation, and I assure you, the "starving artist" myth is one that serves the people who want to take advantage of you. If your belly is empty, you are not going to work at your best, nor will you make excellent decisions, and it won't take much for an exploitative content farm to dangle something in front of you in the hope you'll take a bite. Art needn't be made in discomfort. There is zero shame in comfort, in paying your bills, in *eating food* and enjoying the shade that comes from a *ceiling*, which itself is underneath a *roof*. You may even be likelier to make great art *while* comfortable, because you aren't starving

---

all citizens of this country, bringing us in line with the rest of the first world. Could you imagine all the art that would be made, and the stories that could be told, if we all had that one essential need met without fail? A changed world. Which is why they try not to change it, because they know art and stories are a challenge to power.

or drowning or despairing. Yes, there's certainly a romance to the scrappy young artist, not kowtowing to The Man—but there's also a lot of power behind an artist who can afford some time and space and more than a packet of ramen upon which to subsist. You can do both. You can work a day job and continue to make art. Great art. Your art. Risky, weird, wonderful art.

Art is enough of a risk as it is without you making it riskier.

Have the day job.

Don't starve.

Something Important, Part Three

A REAL WRITER IS ONE WHO WRITES.

There is no other test.

Others will want to test you.

They will make it about how much you write, how often, what you get paid.

But if you want to be a writer, then you write, and you are a writer.

This is the way.

7

The Necessity of Knowing Thyself

WHO YOU ARE AS A WRITER MATTERS. IT'S NOT AN immovable identity; your writer self is not carved into the schist and bedrock of this world so that future archaeologists[1] may unearth it and learn the truth of You. Who you are as a writer doesn't even matter to other people, not really. I mean, fine, it *can*—if you subscribe to any kind of auteur theory regarding the Art and the Artist Who Arted Said Art, then who you are as a writer matters, though even there, who you are as a writer is always something of an invention, an interpretation, in much the same way one reads a poem and gets what they get out of it, even if what they get out of it is wrong.[2] But that's not what I mean.

What I mean is, who you are as a writer matters to *you*.

---

1   I'm betting on octopuses. The Octopod Empire will have great curiosity about the four-limbed skin-monkeys who bumbled and tumbled about this world. Sorry we ruined it for a while, Mighty Octopals!

2   Despite what some English teachers will tell you, some poems really were trying to say a specific thing, and you cannot just freely interpret them to mean whatever you want. What you *get* out of them is yours and yours

Portrait of the Wendig as a Young Man

I did not know who I was as a young writer.[3]

I only knew I wanted to be a writer, and to me, it was simple enough to say, "I want to be a writer." But even there, I'd already hamstrung myself, because I was interested in the end result of the identity, but not discovering the process and the work that leads to that identity. In other words, I really wanted the costume. I wanted to be published. Sure, sure, I guess that meant writing, whatever, blah blah blah, FINE, yeah, I'll write some stuff, but let's talk more about what my BOOK COVER will look like, and ooh, can we talk fonts? Let's talk fonts.[4]

Earlier, I discussed my trunk novels, and they were trunk novels because I was never really working toward understanding what a Chuck Wendig novel should or even could look like. Okay, obviously I understood my name would go on it, but I viewed that more as a trophy and less as a signature—it had nothing to do with who I was, or what a book of mine should really look like. It had everything to do with the accomplishment of it. The cart was so far before the horse I don't think the

---

alone, but what the author intended was—whether they were successful or not—theirs and theirs alone.

3   I mean, not literally. This isn't *Memento*.

4   Okay, I didn't actually mean we should talk about fonts, but while we're here, I always write in Times New Roman, 14-point font, 1.5 spacing; indent the first line of every paragraph by 0.5"; and I do this on a 27" monitor. I do this because I am boring. I know this about myself. It may change, of course. Maybe in five years I'll compose my novels on an iPhone, in Wingdings. Chaos reigns.

horse had even been born yet. I was just someone who really, really liked carts. The horse was an afterthought.

So, when I wrote novels, I did so in a way that was deliberately disinterested in my own input on the matter. I thought I needed to get out of the way, like I was an obstacle to the work. Writing a book meant chasing the current book market—ah, I thought, if erotic space opera locked door mysteries were what was selling, then I should write one of those. (I failed to realize that by the time I could actually write, sell, and publish "one of those," the trend would long have withered and died on the vine, grapes into raisins, raisins into birdshit.) Even when I was hewing closer to genres I actually liked, I was still trying to ape the voices and choices of other authors—the champion folksiness of Joe Lansdale, the humor of Christopher Moore, the character work of Robin Hobb. I was doing my damnedest to be successful by mirroring success: the success of other writers, other books, entire trends of fiction. Needless to say, it sucked. It sucked bad.

It was only when I got selfish that I was able to write a book that mattered to me, and that further was a book that earned me an agent and eventually landed on bookshelves. Fast-forward ten years, and I'm still doing this, holding on to the mechanical bull that is Writing and Publishing as it thrashes about, trying very hard to buck my ass into the mud.[5] And in that time, during that decade, I've come more and more to realize that being a greedy, selfish writer—in the sense that I am utterly self-interested in the kinds of stories that live inside the weird little pulsating nightmare cube that is my heart—is what allows me to keep going.

---

5 Wait, if it's a mechanical bull, why is there mud? You ask too many questions. Shhhhh. Shh.

And so it has become one of my very few, ever-dwindling pieces of advice I give to writers who seek it: know thyself as a writer.

Because it's perhaps the only thing that really matters.

The Singularity of Our Uniqueness

Originality is believed to be important in writing.

It is not.

Or, rather, not in the way you think.

The originality of idea is the first thing we worry about, right? In fact, for writers, *idea* feels like everything. We focus so much on having a good idea, a great idea, a real barnstormin' frogstomper of an idea that it becomes our everything. And we feel like it'll solve *everything*. So we treat ideas as if they are precious gems—if only we could get ahold of one, we could buy the kingdom.

Ideas are empty without a story to go with them.

But ideas aren't gems.

Ideas are costume jewelry.

Which is to say, it's all how you wear them. Ideas are cheap. They're a dime a dozen. Writers get ideas *all the time*. People always ask writers the clichéd question, "Where do you get your ideas?"[6] And I'm fond of saying that the question you *should* be asking writers is, "How do

---

6   I get my ideas from the Idea Machine I built in the deepest Earth. Sometimes it causes earthquakes. Sorry about the earthquakes, but a writer must generate ideas *somehow*.

you make the ideas stop??" Because I'm plagued by them. They're beautiful baubles, and every time I pick one up, I see another one, and I want to grab that one instead—no, wait, *that* one over there, ooh but that one is pretty, too. So pretty. My precious.

Ideas are empty without a story to go with them. It's like having a single ingredient for a recipe but . . . that's it. "Boy, this piece of king salmon looks beautiful. I sure wish I had salt. Or a heat source to cook it." The idea matters, but not as much as what you can do with it. A beautiful ingredient poorly rendered will always fail to stack up against a common ingredient prepared with beauty and skill.

So ideas aren't all that. Their originality is middling.

It's all about the story you wrap around them.

Except there, too, we assume that we can do something *original* with the story, that the core plot and conflict will somehow be unique—devised in a way that has never before been seen.

But truthfully, there's only so much newness you can bring to the table, because stories have been a part of our collective existence since Chug and Grebok painted their tiger-slaying exploits on a cave wall.[7] Though modernity persists, at the end of the day we all come to possess similar emotions and

> *There's only so much newness you can bring to the table.*

---

7   In berry juice and poop, probably. Hey, you work with what you got. Berry juice and poop are probably no less crude than Microsoft Word, if we're being honest.

experiences that guide us through life, and while Write What You Know is incredibly fraught,[8] at the same time, it becomes very difficult, even impossible, to truly write something that is infinitely beyond your ken. We're all using the same colors. There's not going to be a new color. You can't suddenly whip out a crayon no one's ever seen before and say, "This is the color Fripple. It's new on the spectrum. It's somewhere between Charred Prown and Bleak Mordow." Obviously, story elements are more varied than your average splay of colors,[9] but hey, the choices are the choices. You're not likely to invent a brand-new emotion or a situation and conflict that has never before been considered, witnessed, or experienced by another human being.

And that's fine! Hell, it's not only fine—it's storytelling working as *designed*. Stories are *meant* to reflect our experiences, to contextualize our feelings and anxieties and build an empathic bridge between writer and reader. We are *meant* to write about extant things because that's why people care. Fiction helps them see themselves, and others, and the world around that binds or divides us.

So, originality? Not that important.

But!

There is one place where it does matter.

You.

---

8   More on this later in the book.

9   Though to be fair, anybody who has ever bought a brick of crayons for a child or shopped for paint will marvel at the varied panoply of hues, tints, and shades. "Honey, let's paint the nursery in shades of GRAY ENNUI, and the trim can be FROSTED DAFFODILS, or would you rather THE END-LESS VOID?"

You are the *one* original thing that you can bring to the page.

You're it. You're the *fingerprint*, the *snowflake*, the *unique cryptid no one has ever seen before and will never see again.* You are a particular, peculiar confluence of ideas, experiences, anxieties, and emotions that doesn't exist anywhere but inside the wobbly flesh vessel that is your body. No one else has had quite the life you've had. No one else thinks the way you do, not exactly, nor does anyone feel quite the way you feel—oh, certainly they can understand you, but even still, you're always a few inches off-center, aren't you? Just as they are, in a different direction. No one else has that mole on their left buttock, the one that, at night, sometimes grows a single eye and a pair of tiny legs before popping off your rounded ass-mound to run around, scouring the neighborhood for local cats to insult and menace??[10]

No one else has had quite the life you've had.

Point is, you're you.

Nobody else is you.

Which is why it is important to know yourself as a writer, and to seize on that. If you shy away from it—as I once did—you are running from the *very thing* that makes your writing important. If you're going to be just like everyone else and write what you think everyone else would write or read, what's the point? You're fighting the current. The river is you. Know its bends, its rapids. Go with it.

---

10 You thought no one else knew about that, didn't you.

Everywhere You Look, a Dark Forest

It's not just about originality.

Knowing thyself brings another value to the table, too.

Writing, you see, is a dark forest.

Every story, every book, your whole career—dark forests within dark forests. Their size is unknown. Their topography also unknown, because they are ever-changing. The forests contain hidden beasts, deep ravines, thorny tangles, metric buttloads of poison ivy, and probably a murderous hiker or two.

This is why, I believe, when you write a story, you sometimes feel lost within it. As if you are a wandering itinerant who left the safety of the road, and now here you are, in this dark and secret place, trying to find your way out the other side, into the light, toward your destination. And it's why you sometimes feel this way in your career, too, whether when starting out or in its labyrinthine midst—even now I have moments where I feel lost, uncertain, hands out in front of me, taking halting, fearful steps, lest I trip on a root and fall onto a sleeping bear.

It can actually be quite terrifying. I don't lie when I say this feeling can literally stall the breath in my chest and give me an existentially vertiginous teeter-tottering-at-the-cliff-edge vibe. There is a deep cenote in front of me and from this tenebrous pit rises the whispers of many, many fears: this story is bad, no one will read it, no one will want it, your career is over, this is it, game over, man, *game over*. It's like a creative panic attack. And I don't say that lightly.

In fact, consider that, if you've ever had a panic attack before, it sucks. It's not merely disorienting, it feels maybe, just maybe, like you're dying. As a lad with generalized anxiety disorder,[11] I'm familiar with intrusive, insistent panic and fear—familiar with it since I was a kid, honestly. As such, I know how to deal with it. It's like turbulence on an airplane: I know it can come out of nowhere, and I know it feels more terrible than it is, and I know how to talk myself through it and ride it out. But that only happens because I am aware of it. I have self-awareness enough to know the shape and margins of that experience. I gain strategies to cope with it. I know it well, this cabinet of vulnerabilities—from my quirks to my mental illnesses—enough to know when it's normal and when it's not. I even know that anxiety causes heartburn, and heartburn causes anxiety, and the two feed each other in a horrible acidy loop.

We can feel lost in both the writing of a book and in our writing careers.

Since I'm obviously a fan of pouring metaphors over your head like Gatorade onto a winning coach, consider how it is when you move into a new house. First night, what do you do? Stub your toe on something. Hell, that whole first week you might wake up in the night and literally not know where you are. You don't know where anything is. You haven't figured out the house's tricks yet—and the house makes sounds, strange sounds, clicks and taps and groans. But over time, the panic recedes and you come to learn the house. You begin to be able to navigate it in the dark. You learn when a strange sound is just the noise of the house settling after dark, *or* when it's that

---

11   Aka, GAD. Which is also the sound you make while suffering under generalized anxiety disorder. "GAD. GAAAAAD. GAAAAHHHHHHHD."

creepy doll[12] you found in the attic tiptoeing toward your room again. *Or*, think about how it is when you start to learn to cook. At first it's just, "Well, I can make pasta, and even then, it might be gummy." You don't know what's going on. But over time, you learn technique, and more importantly, you learn how to rescue a dish from failure, you learn how to *add* things to a dish to elevate it, and best of all, you learn what the hell you like to eat, and how you like to cook.

Back to the dark forest: If this is your first time lost in the dark forest, it's quite frightening. You may never get out, and should you escape, you may not be so keen to enter it again. Meaning, in writing, you may start a story and never finish it, and if you do, you might decide, "I don't want to do that again." It's scary and uncertain and you don't want to get mauled by a bear, real or metaphorical.

Yet, when you take the time to become familiar with the dark forest, well, it seems a little less scary. You begin to know its contours—and even if it's ever-changing, you can reliably begin to navigate it by its sounds, its smells, the feel of a trail under your feet. You can move faster through it. You know when you're turned around. You're always lost; you can't fix that. But you know how to get *found*. And you know it's not going to kill you. And that's no small thing.

It's not just about knowing the forest. Because the forest changes. It's about knowing *yourself* in that forest. You are the constant.

---

12   How come in horror movies it's some old-ass creepy-ass doll instead of like a haunted Optimus Prime or a passel of demonic G.I. Joes scurrying on the ceiling like spiders?

To speak more plainly and less, well, *metaphorily*[13]—
Knowing thyself as a writer affords you a lot of opportuni-
ties, such as:

a. You can recover from failure more easily and more
   quickly.

b. You recognize what pitfalls and perils are part of your
   process and journey, and what pitfalls and perils are
   not.

c. You more easily can survive those pitfalls and perils—
   because you have survived them before.

d. You come to know your tastes, your interests, your
   ideas, and your obsessions and how they relate to the
   work you're doing.

e. You are provided comfort in the chaos.

Because as you come to know yourself as a writer, you
know why you're doing it. You put onto the page the passion
that brought you there. You allow yourself to be there, in the
story—not directly, of course, but as a series of foot- and fin-
gerprints, pressed into the soft earth of the narrative. You
know what works, too, to align these ideas and thoughts and

---

13 Not actually a word. But it is now, because that's part of the fun of being
a writer. You can just make up a word and now it's real. It's in print. You
can't change it. I did that. I AM A GOD IN THIS PLACE. THE DICTION-
ARY AIN'T GOT NOTHING ON ME.

fears, to tell the tale that needs telling, and further, you come to know the ups and downs of your process.[14] A day of writing, a life of writing, and a career of writing are home to many peaks and valleys. Lots of cliffs you're speeding toward. Knowing yourself as a writer doesn't really remove the cliffs, but it can help you have a creative safety net for when you fall—and it might even help you build a ramp or a bridge to the next ledge.

> *Knowing yourself as a writer doesn't really remove the cliffs, but it can help you have a creative safety net for when you fall.*

Knowing myself as a writer let me write the books that matter to me—and, ideally, the books that matter to you. Because honestly, who wants to read a book that the author didn't really want to write? Why would *you* want to read a book *I* didn't want to write?

Knowing myself as a writer lets my process work—but better yet, lets me persevere when my process fails me.

Knowing myself as a writer tells me when a bad writing day is normal—and when it's not normal. When writer's block is writer's block, or when it's something else entirely.[15]

---

14 An example of this, and I know other writers with similar benchmarks, is that somewhere around the 33 percent and 66 percent mark, I am going to experience the absolute dread certainty that not only is this book terrible, but I'm not even sure it's in English, and to do a kindness to the universe I must quit the Author Life and become a tugboat captain. Thankfully, I have not yet followed this impetus. I am simply aware that these are parts of who I am as a writer. And as an aspiring tugboat captain.

15 More on this later.

Knowing myself as a writer lets me know why I do this, how I do this, when I do this.

Knowing myself as a writer lets me enjoy success and endure failure.

To go back to the cooking metaphor—this is more than just knowing a recipe. It's more than just following a list of steps and ingredients until the dish is done. It's about taste, and technique, and intuition. It's about instinct, but not an instinct you're born with, but rather one you can train. An instinct you can build, over time, with effort. Though at this point I am sure you're asking, even throttling the book, all froth-mouthed and spittle-flecked, your eyes wide and the tendons in your neck popping tight like bridge cables: "HOW?"

How the hell does one Know Thyself as a writer, exactly?

The Advice You Always Get

I'm going to say[16] two words to you now.

These two words are very good advice.

They're also very bad advice.

Most bits of writing advice are exactly that: they are good until they're not, at which point they're bad. Meaning, they work when they work, but tested rigorously, they inevitably fail.

These two words are:

---

16 Actually I guess I'm *typing* them at you. Though in the future perhaps we will invent the technology that allows me to appear next to you suddenly, some kind of bearded holographic weirdo, where I hiss in your ear. Which almost certainly would cause you to soil your corduroys. Nice corduroys, by the way.

"Just write."

It's good advice because, as I'll talk about soon, writing is writing is writing, and if you want to be a writer . . . well, writers write. DO THE THING, I yawp excitedly at you, like a happy golden retriever demanding you throw the ball.

It's bad advice because it is profoundly oversimple and it completely disregards the difficulty of writing, which as I noted earlier, is actually quite hard sometimes. It's like, if you say to me, "I want to learn to play the piano," and my response to you was only, "Then go play the piano," you'd correctly make a face at me like you'd just licked a stinkbug. I mean, what are you supposed to be, Neo in *The Matrix*, having just down-loaded the Piano Program?[17] Have you ever tried playing the piano without knowing how to play the piano? It's all like, BLEENK BLONK GONK. It's horrible. It's a horrible sound. Very embarrassing.

That's because it takes real skill to play the piano.

Just as . . . it takes real skill to write a story.

Now writing a story and tickling the ivories are two sepa-rate things: we are not routinely trained to play music, but we *are* trained to spell words and compose sentences and form paragraphs and, eventually, to write stories. It's generally a part of our education, whereas fostering musical skill may not be. So sitting down and "just" writing is less a BLEENK BLONK GONK moment than it would be if you began pawing at a neighbor's Steinway like a surly cat.

Still, let's change those two words—"Just write"—to some-thing a little different. Let's change them to:

"Practice writing."

---

17   "Whoa, I know Bach's Fugue in G Minor."

Softer. Less urgent. And ultimately, more clear: *just write* has this commandment sound to it, as if you are being told explicitly to go GENERATE CONTENT, but *practice writing* is clear—you're not here for the outcome, you're here for the iteration and reiteration. Practicing is willfully messy; it's you attempting to carve order out of disorder. Practicing is feeling things out, testing your boundaries, less *doing the work* and more *seeing what the hell this even is*. It's simpler. Less pressure at play. There are fewer expectations.

> *You're here for the iteration and reiteration.*

Practicing is definitely more *journey* over *destination*.

And yet, it's still not quite right, is it? Because once again, practicing the piano is fruitless if you don't know anything about playing the piano. And while we are likely given a greater degree of training in writing, it doesn't necessarily make our practice any more fruitful.

So, for clarity and focus, let us add a third word.

Practice writing *mindfully*.

Mindfulness is crucial. But what does that mean, exactly?

Being mindful in general is about awareness and focus. It's not doing something passively, as if it's background noise. But rather, it's about doing it actively—concentrating on it, scrutinizing it, *thinking* about it as you do it.[18] It isn't purely intellectual, either. It's

> *Mindfulness is crucial.*

---

18 Though yes, you can also overthink it! What fun our brains are! A nightmare circus of overthinking it and underthinking it and thinking in the wrong direction entirely!

about how you *feel* when you're doing it. It's about how it might affect others. It's a whole-minded approach, willful and directed.

Consider that one of the "true" pieces of writing advice that gets bandied about, often overly simplistic and reductive, is that writers merely need to do two things to be a writer: write and read. Write and read, write and read, read and write, read and write: an endless loop. Do those things, and a writer ye shall be.

But, again, as with "Just write!" this feels like an underestimation of the work it takes to actually write stories and write them to your own contentedness. Reading is by itself not a particularly illuminating act. If you want to play baseball, you do not osmotically absorb the very concept of baseball just by attending games. That's not to say attending games is without value, but it is not the *attendance* that matters: it's how you spend your time while attending. If you're just leaning back, grousing about how WE NEED A PITCHER NOT A BELLY ITCHER,[19] then you're not really doing much at all. But if you're there to watch, to study, to notice techniques, and to see how far out base runners go before trying to steal a base, or how certain pitchers diversify their pitching styles, or how often the outfielders scratch their crotches,[20] then you're perhaps gaining some measure of wisdom. And that's because you did

---

19 I am sorry for the profanity. I did not mean to cast aspersions on those who need to itch their bellies. I, too, sometimes need to be a belly itcher. Readers should be assured that I will do better in the future.

20 Belly itching may be frowned upon, but in baseball, Crotch Adjustment is a vital skill.

not merely attend, you didn't only *see* the game, you *watched* it, and you watched it actively. Your brain was turned on.[21]

So it is with reading, and so it is with all parts of Knowing Thyself as a writer. You must be an active participant in this. You read looking for skill and technique, for how a writer tells a story, and for how you might tell that story differently—not better, just differently, in the way that is true to you.

Practicing writing is also about doing so with your brain turned on. It's about *participating* in it—that sounds obvious, because if you're the one doing the writing, then how the hell aren't you participating in it? But any action can be done thoughtlessly, passively, with your brainpan turned only to simmer—and that's not always a bad thing. But it's essential to turn that pot to boil and think actively about what you're doing. Be present. Be mindful. Know the choices you're making, know why you're making them, and seek to try different things. Explore. Play. Iterate and reiterate. Mess it up.

Think actively about what you're doing. Be present. Be mindful.

Fix it. Mess it up *by* fixing it and realize you haven't fixed anything at all and so maybe you scrap it but then you can't stop thinking about it so you pluck it out of the bin and now you *really* get your hands dirty fixing it. And all the while, as you're doing this, you're building layers. You're laying down tracks. You're creating *strata* of understanding about who you are as a writer. You see the things that you like, that work for you, that

---

21 I don't mean like "turned on" in an eyebrow-waggley way. Though maybe it was! No judgment. Whatever makes your grapefruit squirt.

you want to do better, that intrigue you and frustrate you and make you want to kick a hole in the drywall. You begin to navigate this old house, this dark forest, this seven-course dinner. You take the time to trust in yourself. To know yourself. To believe that the You who is a Writer *matters*, and you shouldn't run from yourself. We spend so long looking for our voice in other places that eventually we realize we had that voice all along. It was us. And with this revelation, we are free.

Three True-ish Things

THERE EXIST VERY FEW PIECES OF TRUE, UNIVERSAL writing advice.

By universal, I mean advice that applies to every writer, every book, across the board. Regardless of age, genre, career status. I think once I could compile whole lists of items that I considered useful to all, like, *Oh you gotta do this*, and *Don't forget about this*, and *If you're not wearing your Lucky Author Underwear, well, you might as well just flush today's wordsmithery[1] down the crapper, friend*. Certainly a number of writers routinely compile their TEN RULES FOR WRITING, and on that list is usually something about dialogue tags and another something about adverbs and then maybe a curveball about "there must be a dog on page 42" that leaves everyone scratching their head.

But as time has gone on, I've found that those elements I considered "essential pieces of writing advice" turned

---

1   Not a word, but should be.

magnificent colors before withering on the branch and falling to the ground, where once-golden leaves swiftly became mulch.

I've winnowed it to three true things:

1. Writing is sometimes not writing.

2. Writing still has to be writing.

3. You must learn to finish what you begin.

Are these uniformly true? I think so. Are they so generic that they will be of little value to those who behold them? Certainly that's possible, but for my mileage, I think there's something important here in each of these, something of value that may be simple, but *simple* doesn't always mean *obvious*.

Let's unpack.

Writing Is Sometimes Not Writing

Life has trained us that work is about the partnership between effort and result. In chores, you put the dishes in the dishwasher and turn it on, and now they are washed. In school, idle time is viewed as counterproductive,[2] and so we are given worksheets and homework and quizzes and tests, and you

---

2   It's there in that word—*productive*. To produce. And further, we are poisoned by the internet's notion that everything we Produce is therefore Content, a Minecraft-like cube, cobbled together on your digital workbench. If you have Produced no Content, what are you even doing?

must do those things in order to perform well. In work, your boss hovers over you[3] to make sure you're filling out that spreadsheet; a camera and GPS in your delivery van makes sure you're not taking circuitous routes or, *gasp*, wasting any time at all; the ditch isn't dug until you dig the ditch, you lazy sonofagoose. You *do* in order to *be done* and that is the sum total of the experience. If you are not expending that effort and achieving the result, then you are not doing anything at all. Meaning, you are not *accomplishing* anything, and accomplishment is the peak, the pinnacle, the *zenith* of human experience, right?

Ennnh.

Ennnnnnnhhhhhhh.

Writing isn't necessarily like that.

So much of what goes into writing isn't actually writing.

Consider this: A story is a product of you, and you are a product of everything that has ever happened to you up until this very moment in time. Young or old, you are the culmination of your experiences. So, right there, the story that comes out of you is not simply the expenditure of the effort-of-the-moment, but rather, is the peak of a substantial iceberg just barely poking out of the ocean that is you. So, right there, *right out of the gate*, we see that writing isn't just writing. It's living. It's existing. It's being present to write.

> *Writing isn't just writing. It's living. It's existing. It's being present to write.*

And that's just in the abstract.

---

3   Not literally, I mean, unless your boss is Baron Harkonnen.

Writing is also:

Thinking a lot. When I was writing *Wanderers*, some days of writing would just be me . . . thinking. Noodling on stuff. Sitting still and staring into the void and hoping the void tells me how to solve this story problem I'm having. When I run, I think. When I take a shower, I think. When I have to wait somewhere, anywhere, for anything, my brain goes into *story mode* and invisible mind-fingers pick at the stories I'm working on the way my grandmother would pick a chicken carcass for soup.

Then, other days, it was research. That's another time writing isn't writing—when writing is researching everything from bat viruses to local history to artificial intelligence to why my neighbors insist on mowing their lawn thirty-seven times a week.[4]

Writing is reading, too. Not even relevant reading. Just . . . reading. Sometimes it's getting ideas from nonfiction, or marinating your brain in good narrative with great fiction, or making your brain mad by reading a novel that maybe *wasn't* so good.

Writing is a number of writing-adjacent things, too. Outlining. Worldbuilding. A chaotic series of Post-it notes left across

---

4   Okay I'm not actually researching that, but seriously, why? Why are they mowing their lawn so often? It looks like a golf green. Just replace the whole thing with carpet and be done with it. Oh my god, they get this lawn service to come and it's *two* guys on mowers, not just one, and then there's a leaf-blower guy even though it's summer and there aren't leaves and all morning it's VBBBMMMM and VVVMMMWAAAAHHHH and it's dust everywhere and noise and holy crap leave your poor lawn alone the thing is already turning brown because you keep decapitating it every three hours.

your house. Rewriting. Editing. Rewriting *again*. Answering emails. Tweeting.[5]

And sometimes . . .

Writing is quitting.

Yeah, nobody really tells you that part.

Quitting is a part of writing. Not quitting for good, to be clear, but sometimes . . . yeah, no, you have to quit on the thing you're writing. Maybe it's the wrong thing. Maybe it's just not the story you're meant to write. Maybe it's not the story you're meant to write *right now*. You can't quit on everything, but you also have to reject the Sunk Cost Fallacy and realize that continuing to spin your wheels in the narrative mud isn't going to launch you forward.

Writing isn't always writing.

(Of course, the secret here is, nearly all of life encompasses far more than what's written on the label. Schoolwork isn't just schoolwork, sometimes it's studying and talking and, yes, staring off into space. Working your job also means taking breaks and eating lunch, even though your bosses don't want you to do that; it means getting to know your coworkers, it means having all the training and experience it took to get you to where you are now, and so on. The thing is never just the thing. Our days are more than just the minutes in which we exist.

---

5   Okay, tweeting should not be part of your writing process. My hope is that you read this book at a distant enough point in the future that the word "tweeting" doesn't even make sense, and you're like, "Is the author a bird? What is this *tweeting* he speaks of?" I fear the opposite will happen, though, where you'll be reading this book in the future and we will all have the Twitter app permanently grafted to our cerebral cortex [insert *Black Mirror* logo here] [then again, if you're reading this in the future, maybe you don't even know what *Black Mirror* is] [well, shit].

Our days are not just their conclusion, a culmination of what we have completed. Our days are all the days that came before, too. Our minds need time to both train and relax. Writing is like that. So is most of life.)

Writing Still Has to Be Writing

And yet. *And yet.*

At the end of it all, writing is still writing.

All the thinking-thoughts time, all the reading, all the outlining and worldbuilding and experience—it only becomes part of writing when you, well, write it down. You can think about writing all you want—and that *is* absolutely a vital part of it—as long as you *do something with it.* It's like how training for a marathon really only pays off when you . . . run the marathon.

The good news is, it doesn't matter how much, or how often, you write. It's not about *write every day*, or *write two thousand words*. A sentence, a paragraph, ten pages here, one page there—it's still writing. Writing is not writing, except eventually, it comes back around to being writing again.

You Must Learn to Finish What You Begin

You will note I just got done explaining that sometimes, writing is quitting.

And you may further note that these two ideas seem to compete with each other—first, that you should finish what you start, but second, that it's okay to quit what you're working on, thus rendering it impossible to finish what you started, creating what is clearly a writer paradox that will obliterate the space-time continuum and turn us all into free-floating, hyper-intelligent semicolons.

I will explain.

Finishing what you begin is important for a few crucial reasons.

One, because it makes you feel nice. And feeling nice isn't bad. You're allowed to feel good. You're allowed to *pursue* feeling good. And finishing a story? *It feels real good.* You get this little rush of dopamine in your brain,[6] it's wonderful. It feels like conquest. Like eating a fantastic meal you just cooked. It's got this . . . Tom-Hanks-in-*Cast-Away*-Heralding-the-Fire-He-Just-Made vibe. Sure, okay, eventually the feeling might creep in that *oh god I'm not really done this is just a first draft oh no oh shit*, but that's okay, too. That's normal. A feeling of conquest doesn't last forever, nor should it. We always chase the dragon.

Two, because stories are complete items. They are not *beginning, middle, then only endless oblivion*. They are *beginning, middle,* and *end*. The ending to a story is a crucial part of it. Some might even say it is *the* most crucial part, because an unsatisfying or incomplete end will leave a bad taste in someone's mouth—like having a wonderful meal that ends in a dessert of pickled gym socks. You have to learn to do that, and learning to do it means doing it. It doesn't mean doing it well. It just means doing it. So, sometimes, if you begin a thing, you must finish a thing.

Three, because iteration breeds reiteration. Doing something increases your chances of being able to do it again.

---

6   Or maybe it's serotonin. Or fruit punch? Mmm. Fruit punch.

Finishing a story will increase your chances of completing another story, and another story after that. Momentum is created.

Ah, but!

In all writing advice, one must cleave to nuance, and the nuance here is that yes, you must finish something. You just don't have to finish *everything*.

For Every Rule, a Thousand Exceptions

While writing rules are often quite prescriptive, they never really hold up to much scrutiny. Be great if they did, but they don't. For every *hard-and-fast commandment*, there are endless examples of someone who completely broke that commandment and broke it well. Because you can get away with just about anything, if you do it well. And even there, "do it well" is a teleporting bullseye, isn't it? Because though there are certainly some examples of *technically poor writing*, for the most part, beyond that, the rest of how we feel about a piece of work is wildly subjective.

We'll get into more of those so-called rules as the book goes on, but it bears repeating here that rules change with the times—yes, of course, there are writing rules in the sense of how you use periods and construct sentences, though even those are open to some flexibility. Here, we refer more to the larger, squirmier "rules" of writing, rules about adverbs and unlikable protagonists and not overusing wry footnotes.[7] Ultimately, they are less

---

7   Oops.

rules and more preferences or trends, and those change with the winds—changing often, in fact, because some writer or another has chosen to break a rule and break it with aplomb.

When proceeding, it is good to understand these trends and preferences, if only to see why they are in popular use. But it's just as necessary to question them at every step, to be deeply suspicious of anything sold as being *true*. Stories and art do not like to be put into boxes, yet we do it anyway. And inevitably, they break out, they break free, because that is the way of anything born of imagination.

White-Bordered Optional Stop Signs

AS NOTED IN THE PREVIOUS SECTION, AS A WRITER YOU are certain to come across a whole lot of THESE ARE THE RULES FOR WRITING. You will find Elmore Leonard's ten rules, you'll find Vonnegut's rules, you'll find rules from Stephen King and Jonathan Franzen,[1] you will be absolutely besieged by rules. And that's generally how they're framed, too, as *rules*. A rule is, of course, a thing you shouldn't break, *lest there be consequences*. Don't run with scissors. Look both ways before crossing the street. Don't open your mouth until you know what the shot is. Never feed them after midnight. Don't talk about fight club. And for god's sake, don't ever, ever, *ever* use adverbs, or your face will melt off and slide into your coffee and you will die faceless and screaming, you adverb-using *monster*.

---

1   And wow, it's almost like these people have something in common. I can't qwhite imagine what it would be, maybe if I look straight at it, I'll get an answer. If you're abled to figure it out, please e-male me, thanks.

And sometimes I think, gosh, that sorta sucks.

Rules are not gentle. Rules are DO THIS OR BAD STUFF. It's all shut gates and wagging fingers. And that's maybe a little sad, isn't it? Writing is a playground. It's a circus of weirdness, and while yes, the act of storytelling is governed by the need for clarity and momentum, it remains at its best and most interesting when we disable a lot of the limiters and safety mechanisms and see what happens when we embrace a certain kind of

Writing is a playground.

chaos. Chaos both in our process and on the page, because chaos—to a degree, at least—is surprising, it's interesting, it's fun to watch in the way that watching a moose crash his way into a Walmart is fun. You don't know what that moose is going to do. Is the moose okay? Will someone get hurt? Maybe the moose just wants to bounce on a trampoline or eat some Doritos. You're going to keep watching, though, aren't you? Because the chaos of it is suspenseful and delightful in equal portions.

And again, that's not to say writing isn't about imposing some order on chaos—too much chaos feels unmoored, like we can't find a narrative handhold, and if we cannot get hold of a story, it keeps slipping out of our grip and we can find no reason to continue to care. Too much chaos is hard to follow. Clarity is king. And certainly storytelling works often as an act of balancing, unbalancing, and rebalancing, again and again—we show the status quo, we break it, and we keep striving to return to order while simultaneously encouraging chaos to wreck that order.

But how you get there—and how you manifest it throughout—is not exactly beholden to hard-and-fast rules. Or, it shouldn't be. It's not a very enticing way to write. And so I think it's useful here to drag out a lot of the sacred cows of writing—the ones treated like commandments that are trotted out every so often—and give them a spin, see how they look, with the stated purpose of considering that they are, at best, suggestions . . .

And at worst, lies.

"Let's Talk About Adverbs," He Said Adverbially

It's not a particularly dramatic or impactful one, but I think we should start up front with the whole *adverb* thing. Because they all say it. It's always one of the fucking rules, isn't it? NO ADVERBS. NONE AT ALL EVER. ADVERBS ARE A WIZARD'S TRAP. IF YOU USE ONE, YOU WILL BE TRAPPED IN A MIRROR DIMENSION, TORMENTED BY LIVING ADVERBS, WHICH LOOK LIKE BATS FOR SOME REASON, EXCEPT THE BATS HAVE THE FACE OF DAME JUDI DENCH.

This rule, it—

takes a deep breath

It makes me *so* upset.

Because it's really pretty bonkers.

Adverbs are an <u>essential</u> part of our language.

Adverbs modify verbs in the same way adjectives modify nouns. They bring clarity to those words and, in that clarity, also bring us a kind of artfulness—mashing language together is like putting two colors together to create something new, something specific. Sometimes, simply finding the right verb is enough—if I say, *Mortimer ran across the street*, that's one thing. If I say, *Mortimer sprinted across the street*, that implies a little more urgency. But maybe, just maybe, I want something more than that. Maybe I say, *Mortimer sprinted clumsily across the street*, and in adding that adverb—"clumsily"—I'm not only portraying his speedy run, but I am also describing the style and effectiveness of that run. And it tells me a little something about that character in this particular moment of time, contextualized by the rest of the story.

That's super useful!

Why would you *not* want to do that?

And did you know, there are tons of words that are adverbs that you often use and you probably didn't even know it?

In fact, that word "often"? It's an adverb. Specifically, an *adverb of frequency*. In the sentence above, it modifies the verb "use."

Everywhere. That's an adverb of place.

Today. That's an adverb of time.

Almost. That's an adverb of degree.

Above, when I said *clumsily*, that's an adverb of manner, and it also seems to be the singular sticking point with writers who want to chastise you for using adverbs in general, and usually, they mean to chastise you when you use them alongside dialogue tags. Consider these three examples:

1. "Run!" Karen yelled excitedly.

2. "I like cheese," Dave said enthusiastically.

3. "Quack," the duck quacked selfishly.

In number one, the problem isn't the adverb, it's the redundancy. "Yelled" carries enough of its own water that we don't really need to add the adverb. We can assume a yell is, in some way, already an exhortation of excitement.

In number two, it's really down to stylistic choice. It works in part because one does not usually say something so basic with enthusiasm. It lets us know that Dave is a guy who really, really likes his cheese, by god. Now you might change it to:

"I like cheese," Dave said with great enthusiasm.

Or you could simply use the also–occasionally maligned exclamation point:

"I like cheese!" Dave said.

Which is also fine, maybe better, but that's purely down to stylistic choice. Current fiction style probably leans toward not using the adverb, but not necessarily. Some younger-grade fiction seems to hew a little more toward using adverbs of manner in this way. It's fine? It's fine.

In number three, the problem isn't the adverb, the problem is that it doesn't make much sense.[2] How does one say something selfishly? How does one *quack* selfishly?

---

2   Though admittedly, I am now compelled to know what the duck is actually saying. Also, my autocorrect just tried to change "duck" to "fuck," so I feel like I have finally won. I have conquered you, motherducking autocarrot!

> *The problem really isn't adverbs. The problem is either when you overuse them or when you use them in a way that fails to lend clarity.*

The problem really isn't adverbs. The problem is either when you overuse them or when you use them in a way that fails to lend clarity (and may in fact remove clarity). But that's true of *all language*. If you use a noun or verb too much, or you use them incorrectly, yeah, that's a problem. But nobody is putting DON'T EVER USE VERBS OR NOUNS on their silly writing rule lists.

Plus, all the writers frothing about how you shouldn't use them?

They totally use them.[3]

Case closed.

Bang the gavel.

Never Use a Dialogue Tag Other Than "Said"

That's the supposed rule, right? You get one verb for a dialogue tag, and it's "said." Don't change it. Don't mix it up. Other verbs

---

3   To be fair to Elmore Leonard, his admonition to never use adverbs to modify dialogue cheekily includes an adverb ("gravely"), because he's funny and isn't taking this too seriously. Which means you shouldn't take it too seriously, either.

are too fancy, too sassy. Don't get pretentious. Calm down. Said, said, said.

Counterpoint: audiobooks are a thing, and in those audiobooks, saying FRANK SAID, MARY SAID, FRANK SAID, MARY SAID over and over again starts to *chafe the eardrum* a little bit.

So mixing and matching isn't terrible, as long as—like with adverbs—you do not overuse and you try to increase clarity rather than decrease clarity. People are allowed to yell, plead, exclaim, hiss,[4] whisper, all of that. It's fine. Just don't get nuts with it.

Also just don't use "ejaculated" as a dialogue tag.

Not ever.

Please.

I'm begging you.

The Pros and Cons of Pros Using Prologues

Never use prologues, they say.

Except, uhh, well.

Erin Morgenstern's *The Starless Sea* has four prologues. My own book *The Book of Accidents* has by comparison a meager two. *Game of Thrones?* Prologue. *Hitchhiker's Guide to the Galaxy?* Prologue.

Some books have truly exquisite prologues. Essential and fascinating.

Use a prologue if you want. Just make it good, and ensure that it belongs. But again, that's true for everything, isn't it?

---

4   Even without sibilance! That's right, I'm talking to *you*, copy editors.

Even here, I want to tell you my inclination was to add, "Just make sure it's necessary for the story," because that's another piece of well-worn often-waved-about advice, isn't it? But then I want to challenge *that*, too. Because what does "necessary" even mean? Presumably, it means the story cannot be understood without it, but I'll be honest, you could also take any story and rewrite it as an outline of events, a simple beat-sheet detailing the timeline of plot points, and that would allow the story to be told and understood perfectly. But it wouldn't be very *interesting*, would it? So it seems to be the better way to say it isn't so much that it's *necessary*, but that it is additive to the work. A thing exists in a story because it adds something. And the something that it adds is not always an easily definable thing. It isn't just about plot or data. Maybe it adds a character beat. Maybe it's just there for color. I mean, when you paint a room in your house, do you do so because it is somehow necessary for that room to exist? The paint isn't holding up the ceiling. No, you probably painted the room that color because you liked the way it looked. You liked it, so you did it. And sometimes, that's writing. You like it, so you do it.

> *A thing exists in a story because it adds something.*

Use a prologue if you want. Like paint on a wall, it works if it works.

Asshole Protagonists

No unlikable characters, they say.

Bzzt! Bad advice. Unlikable characters are necessary. Besides, what does that even mean? There's not a litmus test for likabil-ity. I think there's a part of us that responds to even the most monstrous characters—from Tony Soprano to Cruella de Vil, we find something to like. It's more a question of livability. Can you live with those characters for three hundred pages, for two hours, for ten issues of a comic book? We need to be able to live with them, alongside them, maybe even in their heads a little bit. And that's okay. As long as they're not boring. There is no moral impera-tive to make every character lik-able. That's not a binary thing.

> *Can you live with those characters for three hundred pages, for two hours, for ten issues of a comic book?*

Likability exists on a spectrum, as do most things. Embrace the spectrum of existence. People are complicated messes.[5] Characters are people. Characters can be messy.

Breaking Rules Is Good for the Universe

Let's pause for a moment and consider something.

The protagonist in most stories is someone who *changes* the world or is changed *by* the world. Change being the con-stant. They are in this story because, as noted earlier, there ex-ists a shift in the status quo—and in some of the best stories, the shift in the status quo is not a product of external plot, but

---

5   Writers, doubly so.

of plot that characters themselves have created.[6] Meaning, the characters are the ones driving the narrative by—whether willfully or without awareness—upending the once-normal situation. They're falling in love with someone they're not supposed to. They're leaving the firelight of the campfire to hunt the beast that menaces the village. They're breaking a prophecy, or running away from home, or defying an empire. They are, quite often, disturbing norms (if not outright shattering them), violating taboos, and, drum roll please, breaking the gosh dang rules.

It is arguably what makes a story interesting—a character has broken some tradition, some plan, some law, and now we're here to find out what that means. They are heretics in some way. They are outsiders.

Our characters are not us, the writers, obviously. Just the same, how interesting do you think it would be if you, the storyteller, followed the rules all the time? If we all did the Top Ten Rules for Writers by Edward P. Sniffington, wouldn't we all be writing the same book?

Telling Versus Showing

Let's tackle a big one.

Show, don't tell.

This is one of the pieces that has good advice at the heart of it but is too short and contains too little nuance to really be

---

6   Remember: Plot is Soylent Green. It is made out of people.

that useful, given how often it is treated like a commandment rather than a gentle suggestion.

The idea, presumably, is that a book that leans too hard into expository language can feel cold, boring, inert. *Telling* means simply declaring a fact, whereas *showing* means demonstrating that fact without telling it outright.[7]

It's about being implicit/covert (showing) versus explicit/overt (telling). An easy example would be:

Telling: John was happy.

Showing: A smile spread across John's face and he felt a lift in his step as he got out of his car that morning.

Is one better than the other? Not really. It becomes very difficult to assess individual sentences this way, though it gets a little easier to evaluate them when you're looking at the whole of the prose. The reality is, most authors will use a mix of telling and showing. Some things will be declarative; others will be described. And that's fine. You can't show everything, because then you're going to just bog the entirety of the work down with language meant to talk around the story rather than just, y'know, *telling the story*. Sometimes, you just want to cut to the chase and ensure that the reader knows exactly what is happening as plainly and as boldly as you can state it. But also you can't tell everything either, because if everything is

---

7   There are some who argue that "showing" in fiction is impossible because it's all words with no visuals and no audio, therefore the whole thing is "telling"—and there's some truth to that, in that storytelling has the word "telling" right the fuck in there, doesn't it? Just the same, I think this is also a little pedantic, and it is safe to assume that showing is how it is described above: not literally painting a picture, but painting a picture with words. Descriptive language, metaphors, all that good stuff.

surface-level explicit text, then there is no chance for subtext, and you'll find less opportunity for ambiguity or uncertainty. And stories sometimes thrive in those margins, so you don't want to eschew them entirely, just as you don't want to keep the story only *to* those margins. A balance is key, and what that balance looks like is ultimately up to the author. You're the one writing the story. You're the divine ruler of this place and you get to decide what gets told and what gets shown.

> *A balance is key, and what that balance looks like is ultimately up to the author.*

In Which I Break My Own Rules Because Fuck It

Of course, showing versus telling leads us into a larger discussion about exposition, and a lot of writers have a lot of very strong feelings about exposition. Most of them, I'd argue, say the word "exposition" the way you might say the name of a nemesis, as if you might spit after.[8] I myself have certainly spoken the rule that the exposition that belongs in the book must sing for its supper, that you only include the exposition essential to the movement of the story at hand—if it does not aid in the forward momentum of the tale, then why include it?

But that's mostly wrong, too. That's just my preference, ultimately, and even in a book of mine like *Wanderers*, there are

---

8   "Exposition? *Ptoo!* Exposition killed my mother. You do not bring up *that* name in this place."

expository bits that are arguably inessential to that story's momentum. I included them (lots of historical and scientific talk about pandemics, for instance) because I thought they were relevant and interesting to the narrative, not because readers literally needed to know those pieces to continue forward. Look at George R. R. Martin's A Song of Ice and Fire series, or any Neal Stephenson novel, and you get ten pages of feast scenes and litanies about quantum mechanics (respectively) and, are those things really key to the story—by which I mean the actual movement of characters through the world? Probably not. Do readers read the hell out of these books anyway? They do.

The desire to slice deep cuts into exposition is, I think, the desire to cut "fat" from a story. But "fat" is not a bad word,[9] and fat represents flavor. A story is not a stainless steel tube pushing nutritive narrative gruel into your mouth. A story is not simply a series of data points to be lined up in a proper order. Stories are strange things, multi-textural. Culinarily, fat carries flavor and offers depth *of* flavor as well, and that can also be true in fiction. Some of the things that may seem extraneous are simultaneously giving us depth and complexity in a way we did not expect. Certainly a work cannot be all-fat, all-the-time, but well-marbled fat renders a tasty meal.

> *"Fat" is not a bad word.*

To carry the metaphor further, because find someone who loves you as much as I love metaphors—a meal is often a lot of different flavors bouncing off each other. Acid can cut the overpowering richness of fat. Bitterness adds complexity to balance against tart or sweet flavors. Adding an unusual ingredient

---

9   Not for people, not for food, not for fiction.

like fish sauce to, say, chicken soup, lends it a surprising depth of flavor that goes beyond mere saltiness and into that mysterious realm of *umami*. And we do this not because this necessarily adds "value" to the dish in terms of the nutrition it provides us—we do it because it helps us enjoy the food more, because we like the competing flavors and the complicating aspects of what we're eating, and sometimes it's the thing that helps us consume and digest the nutritive components. But at the end of the day, we add flavor because we like flavor. Like with the *paint the wall* metaphor from earlier, sometimes we put things in stories because we like them, because we feel those things belong, because it lends the story a kind of narrative richness or because it balances against aspects in the story we have so that they don't overwhelm. (Consider here how a lot of horror writers sharpen the horror by using humor as a counterweight.)

If you want it in the story?

Put it in the story.

It can always get cut later if it adds an off flavor.

The Next Sacred Cow for Slaughter: Write What You Know

Ah! Yes. That old classic—

Write what you know.

Oooh. Mostly bad. Has some good in there. Not entirely useless, but the power of the advice cannot be encapsulated by those four very limited words.

Obviously, the big problem here is when it is framed like a rule chiseled in hard, unyielding rock—because when you take this to be *law*, you can only read it in a way where the only stories you get to commit to paper are ones you have personally experienced. As such, everything you write is at its core some measure of autobiography, memoir, or so-called creative nonfiction. All your "novels" will be barely that at all. And don't get me started on how this impacts genre writers—last I checked, we writers have likely not flown on a dragon, blown up a space station, solved (or committed) a murder, or competed in a brutal set of battle royale games as teenagers to remind us of the infallible power of empire and state.[10] I personally wouldn't have been able to write about all the things I've written about, either.[11] My books wouldn't exist. Most of the books you love wouldn't exist.

Still, the advice perseveres for some reason or another, right? It can't be *entirely* without merit, so what's the point of it?

Here is my take on it:

Write what you know is an opportunity, not a commandment.

The truth is, you know a lot of things. You've experienced a great deal. You have been places, met people, and felt a whole lot of feelings, and there's an opportunity there to mine your limitless depths of experience in a fictional context. No, you haven't experienced everything you are going to write about, but the work can be well served by you trying to find adjacent, proxy experiences in your life. A fantasy character eats some

---

10 Though we're probably closer to it these days than I imagined. Huzzah, encroaching dystopia!

11 Admittedly, we are now living through a global pandemic, but I had not experienced anything like this when I wrote a book *about* a global pandemic, aka *Wanderers*.

strange new fruit after starving; well, no, you've never done that—but certainly you've eaten a meal after being really hungry, you've probably bitten into an apple or a peach or another fruit that was sublime in a way you did not expect. You've never ridden a dragon, but maybe you've been on a motorcycle or horse or even in a fast car with the top down and can at least carry your imagination from that starting point (whipping down the highway) to the exhilaration of riding a goddamn dragon. One of the greatest advantages isn't just looking for sensory details, but emotional ones. No, you've never been betrayed by some kind of Wizened Space Emperor, but maybe you *have* been betrayed by a friend or a lover or a parent, and you can bring that feeling of betrayal into your book—same way you can dig through feelings of love, guilt, fear, what-have-you, so that when your characters experience those things, they feel authentic to you.[12]

Thing is, a lot of this isn't even something you're going to do consciously. You're going to do what a lot of us do, which is *use your imagination to imagine a bunch of cool shit*—but your imagination doesn't come from an empty place. It wasn't here before you. It comes out of all the stuff I'm talking about: your experiences, the people in your life, all your wants and fears and feelings. The imagination is the tree and the life you've lived is the fertile seed bed.[13] You don't have to willfully write what you know. Because that's probably what you're already doing.

> *Your imagination doesn't come from an empty place.*

---

12 And, ideally, to the reader.

13 "Fertile seed bed" sounds weirdly dirty, and I'm sorry.

And! When you don't know something? The advice presents another opportunity: the opportunity to *know more stuff.* Some things you don't want to get wrong. Some parts of a story cannot rely upon pure imagination. When I wrote a book about nanotechnology and pandemics and artificial intelligence, I didn't just make all that stuff up. I researched. I read books. I talked to experts. The things I did not know, I learned. That's not hard. It's not complicated. It's not about getting it all perfect, it's about getting it right enough so that readers feel immersed.[14] When I knew I was going to set my novel *The Cormorant* in the Florida Keys, I went to the Florida Keys. I could've gotten some useful information by just using, say, Google Street View and Wikipedia, but actually being there gave me some useful sensory data—learning about no-see-ums, the tiny biting flies, was something that I got just by going there. You learn how a place smells and feels and pick up curious details from being there—but you can also get to that place just by talking to people who live there. That's okay, too. We can't go everywhere and do everything. We do our best with what is available to us. We bring the ingredients we can to the dish.

So *Write what you know* is perhaps better written as *Write whatever the hell you want to write but anytime you have a chance to bring real-world details or emotions into play, you should feel free to do so, and if there is information that you're missing, go get that information.* But that isn't too catchy, is it?

---

14 My own personal trick to this is relying on something like the game Two Truths and a Lie. If you tell two truths about a subject, then you can make the third thing a lie and the readers will believe it. Because you've already drawn a straight line from those two dots, and the third dot will feel connected and factual even if it is make-believe.

Pretty, Pretty Peacocks

Kill your darlings, the crowd chants. *Kill, kill, kill your darlings.*

A brutal piece of advice. Merciless, and it again stems from that earlier note about the minimalist urge to slice fiction down to its bone—trim every last ounce of fat until it is a lean, osseous *ice pick*. Not that there's anything wrong with that, especially if you're writing something that is meant to be lean, something that needs to get to its point quickly—but it's also weird to suggest this should be your impetus across all fiction.

Here's where I suspect this comes from: when an editor asks for a change or a cut, I suspect they sometimes receive pushback from the author.[15] The editor says, "This shit doesn't work," but the author says, "But I like it." And so engages a small battle between *doesn't serve the work* and *but I like it anyway.* Though this isn't as clean-cut a conflict as one might like, certainly most people would side with the editor, because that's the editor's job. And the author's defense against such a change or cut *can*, in *some cases*, definitely sound like the author trying to protect a piece of the work that they have an emotional attachment to but not necessarily a narrative attachment—it's like having a peacock as a pet in a two-bedroom apartment. That's a big, loud bird, and your roommate is probably mad you have it, because it keeps knocking the PlayStation controllers off the side table with its fancy, colorful ass-feathers, and then it ululates noisily before pooping on the floor of your galley kitchen. And the roommate says,

---

15   I mean, ha ha, *I've* never done this. Ahem. Um. Yeah.

"You have to get rid of this bird, it doesn't belong here," and you say, "But I love him, his name is Mister Purpleton von Preeninghaus." Except your love for the pretty peacock does little to assuage your roommate's irritation over its presence in your tiny apartment. Because it is a loud bird pooping everywhere.

I suspect it's like that. When there's a part of the book that feels like a peacock, strutting around and serving no purpose, they want you to get rid of the peacock. And so the advice is born: kill your darlings.

You love the peacock.

But you must drown the peacock.

For reasons of efficiency.

Except—

Well.

I had a peacock once.

This is not a lie. I grew up on a farm, and very early on in my life the farm was used for Standard Farm Creatures, which is to say, cows and chickens and pigs. But somewhere along the way, we got rid of the cows and pigs and kept only a few chickens and then, soon after, began to host an increasingly unusual menagerie of animals. Our big thing was whitetail deer—we started with two[16] that we raised in the house for their first year, and who were truly like pets. By the end we had thirty-six of them. But we had other odd animals, too: rabbits, elk, some albino pheasants, and, in fact, a peacock.

The peacock served no great purpose. Who gets a peacock for any purpose? They don't have any. They're peacocks. We

---

16 Flower and Rudy, if you care to know their names.

weren't going to eat it.[17] It wasn't unfriendly but it wasn't friendly, either. It didn't know how to mow the lawn, and it couldn't help me with my math homework, so it wasn't contributing very much at all. Mostly, it ate bird feed, it wandered around with its rainbow ass on display, and it yelled a lot in a singsongy, screamy-yelpy sort of way.

But it was cool.

We liked the peacock.[18]

The peacock didn't bother us. The peacock looked cool. The screamy peacock yells were not bothersome, and in a way, made us feel like we were at the zoo. Which, in a sense, we were. Y'know, because of the peacock.

If we had gotten rid of Jerry because of his lack of utility, then I like to think our lives would've been a little less interesting. Maybe the beauty and peculiarity of the bird *was itself* a kind of utility, if a kind that isn't often well-favored and well-considered.

The problem, as I've said before, is art ain't math. It may use math in the making, but it's good to remember that art and storytelling are not plug-and-play. Not everything is down to numerical, cold precision. Sometimes the peacocks stay because the peacocks are pretty, and that's okay, too.

Which is the first concern with the advice that calls for you to kill your darlings. If something truly feels out of place and contributes nothing, I think it is worth considering taking that

---

17   Can you eat a peacock? I mean, I guess technically you can eat anything, but I've never gone to the grocery store to buy a pound of ground peacock or a pair of bone-in peacock thighs.

18   You're going to ask the peacock's name, and I confess, I forget. Let's call him "Jerry."

something and saving it for a story where it can belong—a better home. The peacock in the kitchen is a problem. The peacock in a farm, while still *odd*, isn't a problem at all. But also, sometimes? As reiterated elsewhere in this book, if you like it, you like it. And if you really feel that way, then trust your gut, and keep it when you can keep it. There is a gentleness and affirmation to saying, "I want to keep this because I love this."

That leads into the second concern with the advice—it's often misconstrued to mean something even worse:

If you love something, it is a darling, and must be killed. Choke it.

And that makes no damn sense at all.

The things we love in a work already have that one thing going for them: your love of them. We certainly shouldn't be on the lookout for the pieces of a story that we feel strongly about just to axe them from the work.

Storytelling to me is an act of love and an exhortation against loneliness. Writing and storytelling are a call-and-response to the world. It's you saying, I love this, I care about this, I need to talk about this, and I hope you love it, too, I hope you care about it, also, and please hear what I want to say. It is a plea to the universe that the story finds someone else like you out there. Someone who wants to hear what you have to say, who wants to love what you have given them, who likes the same weird things you like. Because here you are, building these massive empathic bridges from author to theoretical reader. And you build those bridges out of the parts of yourself

Writing and storytelling are a call-and-response to the world.

that you feel desperate to share. So to take special effort to find those things only to execute them brutally—why? Why kill the things that make the work yours?

Again, I want to be cautious here not to suggest that anything you put down in a story is somehow sacrosanct and not subject to editing. Stories are often *made* in their edits. Sometimes the editorial process is intensely delicate—I often compare the editing work that went into *The Book of Accidents* to a rewiring of sinew and capillary. Sometimes, editorial is taking a chainsaw to the draft to lop off all those awkward limbs that are just getting in the way. Your love of a thing doesn't mean it's not in some way hampering its effectiveness or bloating the work—and to reiterate, I am fairly certain that is the origin of this piece of advice. So, to counter it, I offer its opposite—

If one is expected to kill their darlings . . .

Know which hills to die upon.

Then one must also be expected to know which hills to die upon.

Meaning, it's your book. It is your name below the title. You have to stand by it, and if you feel strongly about keeping something—even if that something feels like it's a so-called darling—then you must know that this is a hill to die upon. Obviously the whole book can't just be graveyard hill after graveyard hill, because the goal is *not* to die on any hill, really. But you also have to know that if you're going to keep something, you know why. The point here is, it's okay if that reason is something more ethereal, ephemeral, or ambiguous than desired—sometimes it isn't, "Well, this is vital to the plot," or, "This tells us something about the character's backstory." It really can be just, "The peacock is here because I want a peacock here." That's okay, too. It is an act of self-love[19] to be able to say those things about your work and to keep the parts of it that make it yours and yours alone.

Ageist Piffle

You have to be published before [insert needlessly early age here, usually around thirty-five] or you must become a tax accountant.

Pshhht. Pfft. Ageist piffle!

There exists no deadline to become a writer. You can publish at age twenty-five or seventy-five, just write the best book you can write. So many writers didn't start publishing until their forties, fifties, even sixties. It's fine. You're good.

Talent Versus Skill, You Can't Be Taught Writing, Blah Blah

I hear this too often, that talent is everything, that writing isn't a skill, that it can't be taught.

And that makes me want to scream.

Okay, first let's talk talent.

Is talent real? I don't know. Maybe. Can you measure it? No. Can you practice it? I don't know. The idea here is that some people are more inclined to be "good" at a thing than other people, and I often wonder if really talent is just how

---

19   Er, not that kind of self-love. I mean, probably, I haven't read your book. Just leave the peacock out of it.

some people are more inclined to *like* a thing, and as such, they do it more and therefore build up their abilities around that thing. So in terms of writing, it's less that someone has talent or aptitude and more that they have interest, and in having that interest, they pursue it more doggedly, because obviously we pursue the things we like. And so, they get better at it.

Further, even if talent *is* real, it's meaningless without effort. To be quite frank, I've known a number of people throughout my life who have been very talented writers and who, for a variety of reasons, never really applied that talent in a meaningful way, and are ultimately not writers anymore. Talent as a metric is pretty worthless. Writing is a skill, storytelling is a craft, and both can be taught, which is to say, both can be *learned*. And they can be learned at any age, and applied at any age, which brings us back to the ageist piffle noted above—often the ideas about how writing is born of talent and cannot be taught are myths used to make people feel good. If I, a published writer, can say, *it is because of my talent that I am here*, that makes me feel good, and it identifies me as special, and it suggests that those who are not published writers are therefore lesser and not special. It's the same way that some people want you to believe who is a "real" writer and who is not, who are literary darlings and who are just hacks, and it's all a way to slice-and-dice us up into an entirely imaginary hierarchy. Don't buy into it.

Lightning Round

Let's whip through some of these:

Never use the word "suddenly." Unless you want to. Just don't do it too much, c'mon. It's like exclamation points. It's a strong spice, is all.

Skip the boring parts. Good advice in theory, in that, if you're boring yourself, maybe you're boring the readers. But also writers are a particularly bad judge of their own work, especially as they're writing it. And we can be down on ourselves a lot, too, serving as our harshest critics. Be cautious with this one. I think it's less about skipping the boring parts, and more about cutting them. It's editorial advice more than writing advice.

Give us a character to root for. Paraphrased, that's a Vonnegut one, isn't it? Not bad advice, but also drifts closely to the *must be likable* commandment.[20]

Every character should want something. Another Vonnegut, but also pretty common. Not bad advice, again, but maybe a bit simplistic—I think there are a lot of portals into a character. Their wants, fears, and especially their problems. Problems can define a character and a story.[21] A character like Tony Soprano—well, I couldn't tell you want he wants, but I can damn sure tell you about his problems, and those are compelling even if we do not particularly like him.

Open your story with action/don't open your story with action. Well, which is it? If ever there's proof that writing advice is bullshit, it's that I've seen both of these paraded about as gospel truth. For my mileage, opening with action is fine, but we also need context for characters in that action—it shouldn't simply

---

20 Also, if this rule were law, a TV show like *Succession* could not exist.

21 And here is where I shamelessly show my peacock feathers and remind you that you can learn more about this in another of my writing books, *Damn Fine Story*, which you should go out and buy immediately, I say, trying to hypnotize you with the magical power of footnotes. Did it work? Hm.

be characters we do not know and cannot yet care about Doing Exciting Shit. Action works because we care about the stakes of that action, and opening with raw action can rob us of some of those stakes, because it forces the stakes to be shallow— what we really care about is character, who they are and if they're okay, or if they're able to achieve what they are trying so hard to achieve. So opening with action is fine, but you also have to be savvy enough to give us a reason to care about the characters in that situation, even if it's done in a merciless and brutal fashion.

Don't open a book with weather. The cliché of this being, it was a dark and stormy night, right? I dunno. It's pretty weak advice, isn't it? Opening on weather can be overused or clumsy, but that's more on the writing than on the choice. Open with weather if the weather is relevant.

Don't open a book with a character regarding themselves in the mirror. I totally did this and it was fine. Like with all things, don't overuse it. But you can do it. It's not even that weird, is it? Actual human beings look in the mirror all the time and use such a moment to regard themselves in a way that goes beyond just checking out a few blackheads or nose hairs.

Avoid passive voice. Good baseline level advice because passive voice often lacks confidence and authority. But sometimes, it works, too. Passive voice can bring a little bit of rhythm to a sentence, it can highlight action over the actor, it can make a thing sound high-minded and even a bit satirical. Use sparingly, but that's not to say never at all.

Avoid [insert some element of grammar here]. Avoid run-on-sentences or sentence fragments or em-dashes or semicolons or blah blah blah. I don't know that you really need to *avoid* them as if each is a plague upon your book. Maybe you also don't need to marinate the book in them. But then again, hey, you read some Cormac McCarthy or James Joyce, shit gets pretty cuckoo in there.

The only thing you need to do to be a writer is to read and to write. Nice advice at the core—writers write, and further, writers must be readers. A writer who isn't a reader is like a surfer who can't swim. But it's also limiting to say that this is *all* you have to do. As noted elsewhere in the work, the goal is to write and read with intention and mindfulness, and further, a good writer also lives life. They note their experiences. They internalize those experiences, they meet people, they explore their world. I think those are good for you as a human, and that makes it good for you as a writer, too.

Never-Ending Chestnuts to Roast

There's more, of course. Always more.[22]

The point is that the work is yours, and it is a great kindness to yourself and to that work to care less about the rules of writing and care more about the rules of writing *the book in front of you*. Every book is different. I've broken rules and found it useful to do so.[23] I've put things in my books that were definitely darlings, that on paper, under scrutiny, might not belong—but that were still some of my favorite parts of those

---

22 Hell, Franzen's list suggests no one with an internet connection ever wrote a good novel, and I'm like, the internet is essential to my process? Are my novels terrible? Wait, don't answer that.

23 I am fond of saying, "We learn the rules to know when to break them, and we break the rules to know why we needed them in the first place."

books. I've read whole chapters in other people's books whose existences I could not justify in the sense of their plot-essential inclusion, but that I loved maybe more than any other chapter. Sometimes, we are going to talk about weather. Sometimes a character will regard themselves in a mirror.

It's not to say there's no value finding what the supposed "rules" are at any given moment in time. It's worth identifying them to see what value they bring—to try to break them apart in your hand and find the precious stones within.

The rules aren't really rules.

But the rules aren't really rules, as noted. They're preferences, trends, desires. If you read older novels, you will find a lot of the supposed "rules of writing" to be broken on every page. Time moves on. Trends shift.

As noted, so-called rules are also the product of survivorship bias—*I avoided this, and I was successful, so you should avoid this, too.*

But there is something bold about saying, *This story is this way because I need it to be this way,* even though it deviates from some supposed norm. It can be courageous to leave the firelight and walk into darkness—even though we know that darkness is where monsters lurk and pits await. It doesn't mean you're always right. But it does mean you sometimes need to try it. You need to step out of the light. You need to walk into shadow. Because that's what's calling you.

Writers sometimes need to listen when the shadows call.

So break the rules if you must.

Because they're not rules. They're not carved in stone—they're drawn in wet sand, and as soon as the sea comes, they'll be gone again anyway.

Something Important, Part Four

FAITH IN THE WORK IS NOT ESSENTIAL TO DO THE work.

Do the work. Trust in the power of the act.

10

You Are Not Alone

ONE TIME AT A WRITING CONFERENCE, A HUGE AUTHOR, a great author, one whom I shall not name for fear that you will think I'm slagging this author, said that you shouldn't really be friends with other writers.

You should, he said (and I'm paraphrasing here), be friends with, like, *regular people*. Plumbers, boxers, lawyers, whoever. The idea, if I recall, was that making friends with normie, non-writer-folk grounds you a little bit. It ensures that you're not just flying high in the clouds of writer-land, huffing muse-farts and whatever.[1] You break free of your creative echo chamber bubble, and it reminds you that there's a world out there you're writing for, and writing about.

I don't think this is *bad* advice, precisely. I think you should definitely be friends with non-writers, too. For some of the reasons noted above, but also because being friends with one type

---

1   Okay, I'm *really* paraphrasing here. He did not say anything even close to the phrase "muse-farts."

of person from one type of career doesn't sound particularly interesting, and life is a buffet, so sample its wares.

But I also know that, on the other side, you should *definitely* have friends who are other writers.

As noted earlier in the book—the harsh writing advice that set this whole thing off, in fact—sometimes people believe that other writers are your competition.

This is untrue.

Other writers are your community.

Other writers are your community.

Writing is an ultimately lonely, isolated[2] job. I don't need to describe it for you, but just so we're clear, at this very moment I'm in a shed in my yard, hunched over a keyboard, totally alone, as I write this book. And this is me, for hours and hours on any given day. I don't hate it. I like it! But if it weren't for my family, there's really no guarantee I'd eat food on a meaningful schedule, or sleep, or, like, wear pants. I'm already ruined for public life, but without them, I suspect I'd have gone feral a long time ago, sleeping in a nest of shredded manuscripts and hissing at the moles and voles I've collected in a bucket for my breakfast.

It's not healthy to be isolated for so long.[3]

And I think there's a larger isolation, too, if you choose not to be friends with other writers. Because, to be honest, nobody really understands what writers do except other writers.

Have you ever spoken to the Normals about writing?

They say: "Oh, what do you do?"

---

2   And isola*ting*.

3   All work and no play makes Chuck a very dull boy.

And you say: "I'm a writer."

That's when something happens.

They maybe give you a look, and that look is possibly total bewilderment, or utter dismissal, or weird excitement.

A look of bewilderment means they don't know *what* that means. You could've told them, "I'm a zebra farmer," and you'd get the same look. "Oh, that's nice," they will respond, and then walk away.

A look of dismissal suggests they think you're a "writer" with the most vigorously sarcastic air quotes imaginable. *Sure you are*, their gaze says. *Suuuuuure*. They view you as some kind of bottom-feeding suckerfish sitting in your mother's basement writing your weird stories for an audience of three, one of which is you, one of which is your mother, the third of which is a red panda who has learned to use the internet in his zoo enclosure somewhere.[4]

A look of excitement is in many ways the most troubling of all, because this person overestimates all aspects of what you just told them. It means they're going to, in short order, spew to you one of the following:

a. Tell you a book idea they had, and you can write it, and in their magnanimity, they will split the money with you, fifty-fifty, wow, whatta deal;

b. Ask if you know Stephen King or some other hugely successful author;

---

4   The red panda's name is Commander Twinkles and he LIKES THE THEMES OF MY WORK, OKAY.

    c. Assume you wrote a movie, or had a movie made of your books, because we all know a book only truly exists when it is on a movie or television screen;

    d. Assume you're profoundly wealthy[5];

    e. All of the above.

This extends even to people who understand it more—my wife has long had to put up with my blather about writing and publishing, and she is a good listener and knows how to ask questions and is not without some knowledge of both the creative process and the business side of it. But there's still a point when I can tell, okay, I've lost her. A tiny moment of missed focus. It's not her fault, because holy crap I am almost certainly way in the weeds and am dragging her down into the boring publishing muck. But you can tell: I've gone too far afield and she no longer has any sense of the horizon.

Ahh, but have you ever talked to another writer?

Oh! Ohhh. Oh my *god* it feels like you're being *seen* and *heard* for the first time. Our writer problems may be First World, but they're still problems, and to have someone actually comprehend them in some way? It's like *cake*. It's like cake when you've been starving. Like it's your first piece of cake after never having had cake before in your whole life.

It's an amazing thing to be heard and understood. And it's an amazing thing to be there for another writer in the same way. Especially because as writers we don't have any naturally

---

5   Hahahahahahhaaaahahahaha no

occurring communities available to us. We don't automatically gather in a workplace setting. Conferences and conventions are an option, but not only are they once or twice a year, they can also be expensive and require extensive travel to attend. The best we have is social media, and that's both a "thank god for this refuge" and an "oh no this bird-site is not a refuge, it's a Hell-realm." Communities of writers are formed with purpose, not by proxy, not by default. Some of my best friends are writers, or are folks inside publishing. And they grok me and the things I'm going through, whether it's creatively or professionally, more than the average person.

I can go to a writer friend and I can complain about edits or ask about an editor. Or I can whine about, I dunno, some bad review I got, or I can celebrate one of the good reviews instead. And other writers can do the same with me. It's *nice*.

And nice is in short supply, so get you some, immediately.

Still, as with all things, there is a dark side, and it is also a kindness to yourself to be aware of some red flags:

Not every relationship is a good one, and certainly relationships with other writers can fall into that category as well. Now I'll say up front that I believe, perhaps in a very *biased manner*, that quite seriously most of the writers I know are actually really lovely people, and I've been fortunate enough to know a great many who I'm glad to know. But sometimes, you might end up in a relationship that is in some way toxic, and it's important to protect yourself there, too. If you need writer-specific signs of such a relationship, they might include (but are not limited to) things like:

- Professional jealousy, perhaps weaponized against you in some way

- The opposite, which is to say, holding power over you or attempting to make you feel small (or the worse version, attempting to actively keep you down)

- Using you, always asking for help and favors but never returning them (relationships should not be a one-way street)

- Gaslighting you into believing the things you know exist are not happening

- Attempting to poison you[6] against other friends or professionals (this is a sign of narcissism and is a big ol' red flag waving)

That's not to say these aspects cannot be overcome. Nobody's perfect, and writers in particular are like weird cats.[7] But you also don't owe anybody anything, especially your time and emotions in a toxic situation. I am not a relationship counselor, but in my view, there's little reason to cling to a bad relationship, whether you're a writer or not. No sunk cost fallacy needed. Do yourself the favor and be free, little bird.

It's also worth noting that sometimes, groups of writers can be problematic. Some online groups can go toxic, and certainly some critique groups can have some bad vibes baked

---

6   Er, not literally poison you. Though, if they try to do that, that's also very bad?

7   You know what I'm talking about. Stares at ghosts, probably. Wants attention, then hates the attention you just gave. Will disappear for days and return as if nothing ever happened.

into them. In these cases, with organizations and groups that are less purely friend-based and are more professionally focused, it's important to keep your eye on your own work and career and ensure that whatever's happening in the group is there to help everyone, and if the group is not functioning for you or for them, it is fine to politely disentangle yourself. Again, writing is an isolated job, and it's important to ensure you have that

Keep your eye on your own work and career and ensure that whatever's happening in the group is there to help everyone.

community—*but*, if some part of a community isn't working for you, you can return to it being a relatively isolated job without it hurting the work. Because that *is* the work.

It's important to realize—in how you treat other writers and how you hope they'll treat you—that we're not rungs on a ladder. We are not an expendable resource. There exists this persistent, pernicious notion that a writing career is about Who You Know, that if you schmooze the right author, editor, or agent at a bar, they'll slip you a publishing contract under the table and toss you the keys to the Publishing Elevator. I got an agent by doing it the old-fashioned way: submitting a query letter, then a manuscript when asked. And most of the writers I know? They did it the same way. And those who didn't found some other oblique angle—they didn't buy an editor a pony.

That's not to say your relationships won't help you. They can, and will. That's the nature of community. But it's also not a *requirement* of it, and a healthy community is not one that is designed to be transactional but rather one that exists because . . . well, you like the people in it. It's not about farming deals or currying favors, it's just about having people to whom you relate and who can relate to you, in turn. And then sometimes, those relationships and communities will pay off in different, more professional ways. This isn't to say publishing is a perfect meritocracy. It isn't. It is often bogged down with systemic biases and certainly there exists some measure of transactionality. But for my mileage, the thing you can control and the thing you can count on is writing the best thing you can write. Rely on the work, and not on human-shaped ladders.[8]

We must consider our own needs and the needs of our community. We are best served when we leave a ladder out and a light on for those coming up behind us, and hopefully, someone has done that for us as well. Ultimately, it's just nice to be a part of some kind of community of people who get what we're going through. Writers need to be complete creatures, and you can't just be facedown in a puddle of your own work for the remainder of your existence. We, like video game Sims, have a whole catalog of needs, and even we introverts still need social interaction at times to fill up those satisfaction meters above our heads. So it's important to form those relationships and ensure that those relationships are healthy and happy. Be good to yourself. Be good to others. And demand they be good to you in return. It really is as simple—and as complicated—as that.

---

8   Or would it be ladder-shaped humans? Hm. This is some real *Human Centipede* business to consider.

11

Genre Is Just Some Shit Somebody Made Up

THIS BOOK YOU'RE HOLDING RIGHT NOW BEGAN LIFE as a very different book about storytelling in genre.

The goal was to take some of the lessons and notions put forth in *Damn Fine Story* and extrapolate them out across various genres.

I thought I would take each genre—horror, mystery, sci-fi, fantasy, all the fiddly little subgenres!—and talk about each genre's touchstones and about how one can use those elements in storytelling. But even as I started to pick it apart, every aspect I expected to be a straight shot to a conclusion ended up being a maze with a lot of switchbacks, loops, and dead ends. Every genre is puzzlingly, frustratingly inexact in how it works and how it compares to other genres—and that's before you start to drill into the bedrock to unearth a lot of the fiddly little subgenres and the catalog of tropes. Like, okay, fantasy and science fiction are both genres, yes, but ultimately they are *setting*-based genres dependent largely on whether your worldbuilding relies more on magic (fantasy!) or science (sci-fi). But then there's Star Wars, which is ostensibly both, in that it has spaceships and planets and hyperspace, and it also has Jedi mind tricks and dragons and Dathomirian witches. And, further complicating things, you could totally tell a murder mystery in Star Wars, thus introducing a third axis, and that murder *mystery* could itself be a kind of *political thriller*, and because there's *murder* in it, maybe there exist scenes of *horror*, and because it's Star Wars, maybe it also contains *romance*, aaaaaand that's where my head melts into bubbling slag.

It's not that this is a bad thing. It's a good thing. It is even a thing, one could argue, that is deserving of a *whole damn book* dedicated to its intricacies, which was part of the point of writing it.

This just isn't that book.

Why, though?

Well, because for me, the pandemic shifted around a lot of things,[1] and one of the things it shifted around was, as I was writing *that* book, an entirely different book emerged: a book about being good to yourself as a writer, and part of that was how we need to challenge more of our expectations about both the writing life and the act of writing and storytelling itself. I am at a stage as a writer—and I'm seeing this in other authors too—where we are routinely holding up the things we once viewed as important or necessary in our work and saying, Is this as important or as necessary as we once imagined it to be?

Genre is definitely a part of that, because genre is a thing someone just made up. Genre[2] is something of an unstable,

---

1   The epilogue to this book will get deeper into this subject.

2   From the French, meaning, *who the fuck knows, I don't know, you don't know, bah, let's eat stinky cheese and drink wine instead, mon frère.*

untenable taxonomy of literature—complicated even more so these days since it tends to be just slightly pejorative, meaning anything that isn't Literature, or Fiction-in-General. When we say *genre* we expect that it must certainly indicate something without much—nose in air, pinkies out—*literary merit*. Which of course is epic bullshit. Genre is no less than literary fiction, and literary fiction is no less than genre, and just as fantasy and mystery can have a baby, and so can sci-fi and horror, it is perfectly acceptable for your *genre novel* to be *also very literary*. Those terms get incredibly muddy, particularly when you realize all this talk is mostly marketing-speak. It's designed to help bookstores and libraries know where to put books on shelves so that it funnels readers who want a specific type of story to those particular types of stories. There's nothing wrong with that, of course. Readers want what they want and their quest to find those things should be rewarded with ease of discovery.

But that's not to say it's a very good way to *write*.

It can be. No harm, no foul in someone who wants to very explicitly write a story that follows all the genre traits and tropes that go with a specific type of story. You can, if you so choose, intentionally write a novel that is meant to go on one specific shelf at Barnes & Noble. Mystery! Young Adult! I think they have a horror shelf again, which is wonderful, so—yeah, there's another. Horror! But I also know that a lot of today's writers (such as myself) grew up gorging ourselves on every genre under the sun. (And as such end up writing stories in weird microgenres like "time-traveling bird horror" or maybe "dystopian ghost erotica.")

Once upon a time, my mother mostly read one type of

book: thrillers. That's pretty much it.[3] Now I find that readers are less married to one type of genre over another,[4] so we are likelier to take two action figures from two very different storyworlds, mash them together, and say, NOW YOU KISS. We love blending genre. It's both because it's fun and it's also because sometimes storytelling is an act of overturning the pitcher that is our brain and seeing what pours out. We put a lot into that pitcher. And it rushes out in a messy, joyful splash.

Here are some examples from my own work:

I wrote *Blackbirds*, in which Miriam Black can see how you are going to die when touching you, as a genre mash-up of *horror* and *crime* fiction.

It was published by its first publisher as *urban fantasy*, despite not containing many of the hallmarks of that genre, and also, not being urban at all.

When that publisher lost the rights, a second publisher picked it up and still didn't want to call it *horror* or *crime*, so they called it *supernatural suspense*. Which, ooookay, isn't exactly wrong, but it also isn't exactly an established genre.

Some *reviewers* of that book reviewed it as if it were a Young Adult novel, which it is most decidedly not, because the protagonist is not a young adult, and the topics contained within are not relevant to a teen audience, and because the book is filthier than the floor in a strip club men's room.

---

3   In fact, to trick her into reading my novels, I considered using a permanent marker to write ROBERT LUDLUM on the covers. Thankfully, she was actually very nice and read my books anyway, because she was a wonderful mother.

4   Though again, no judgment if you really only read or write one thing. You do you.

My novel *Wanderers* is a peri-apocalyptic epic novel that is . . . what, exactly? A lot of reviews called it science fiction, which is fair. It was nominated for the Bram Stoker Award, which is an award for horror novels. Some blurbs suggested it was like a Michael Crichton novel that had a baby with a Stephen King novel. Crichton did not write horror, and King does not write science fiction, except they both totally do. *Jurassic Park* is totally a monster-based horror movie. *Under the Dome* is very sci-fi.

My latest, *The Book of Accidents*, was explicitly written as a horror novel and contains what I feel is zero percent science fiction, but plenty of reviews have suggested that it is at its heart a sci-fi novel. Are they wrong? No. Of course not. Because genre is a box of motley LEGO bricks. Genre is not without meaning, but it is often without rigor in that meaning.

By which I mean it doesn't have to set the course for writing whatever it is you want to write. Stories are wiggly. They don't necessarily conform to one thing over another—they certainly resist easy categorization, often trying to leap every fence and obstacle you place before them, like angry horses. We *feel* like we must buttonhole a book into a single genre because publishing and marketing suggest we do. And yes, certainly there's value in figuring out what genre our book is going to be shelved under, though ultimately that's not going to be your decision anyway. And that doesn't mean *writing* the book to conform only to one genre and its set of respective tropes—it just means that when asked to, you should be able and willing to drop it into one genre box after all is said and done.

But there's also a different aspect here—asking for your story to be put in a particular box, a box marked THIS GENRE or THAT GENRE, a box full of certain tropes and characteristics, is also akin to asking for permission. Genre is decided outside of us, but by trying to get a story to conform to it, it serves as an act of us shaping the work to fit predefined expectations.

We operate best when we cease asking permission.

As authors, we operate best when we cease asking permission.

Permission is good and necessary in much of our daily lives, especially those interactions and intersections that require the consent of other people. But art is yours. The story isn't an interaction with anybody—not yet, at least. It's something born from the womb that is your heart.[5] We shouldn't write defensively, back on our heels, backed into a corner. We shouldn't feel like we have to mold a story into a particular shape so it can neatly slip into a clearly marked envelope. Sometimes, you just gotta say, "I am going to put some motherfucking peanut butter in this motherfucking chocolate."[6]

Holy hell, could you imagine if someone told George Lucas, "Hey, this sci-fi movie has too many space wizards. Can you cut these goofy magic powers?" Or Ridley Scott, "This sci-fi movie feels too much like a horror movie. What, are you trying to tell a haunted house story on a spaceship? Get it together, buddy. Pick a lane." Try stuff. Write what you think sounds

---

5   Okay that's a really weird image, but I'm going to leave it.

6   Or mayo, peanut butter, sweet pickles, and bacon, toasted in the oven with American cheese melting on it. It's an excellent sandwich and I dare you to try it. I call it the CHNURK MANDOG. Eat it now. Report back. Just trust me on this one. Have I steered you wrong yet? Don't answer that.

great. Write the things that interest you, even if those interests span the gaps across various ill-fitting genres. "I want to write a mash-up of *The Terminator* and *Gilmore Girls*. With a little bit of *The Great British Baking Show* and *Midsommar*." Go for it! I want you to do that because *you* want to do that. We get one life to live. Don't feel like you have to beseech the publishing gods for permission to do it.[7]

And this goes beyond genre, ultimately. Into format, into topic, into point-of-view or narrative tense—life is short, write what you want to write. Write what you *need* to write. Yes, whatever it is, it has to work. It has to be good. But that's true of anything you write anyway. Look at it this way: the mechanics of good storytelling remain true across the board.

To put it differently—

Dolphins have finger bones.

And here I imagine you're saying, "Is Chuck Wendig stroking out? Is he in danger? Do we need to do a wellness check on him?"

I assure you, I am fine.

But I must repeat and reassert:

Dolphins have finger bones.

(Or, put more creepily, *Dolphins have hidden fingers.*)

Let me explain.

If you were to hold up a dolphin, and then hold up a human, no one would confuse one with the other. Not even if you

---

7   I'll note here that there is a sticky wicket when it comes to issues of cultural appropriation and stories of "own voices"—this is not a clearly defined space with easy rules, and I am not at all the person best suited to explain it, or even a person whom you should really listen to in this matter— but in this, a vigorous Google search should help you see the issue at hand.

put a baseball cap on the dolphin.[8] A child would know the difference.

But, if you were to X-ray both of them . . .

Well, okay, you still wouldn't confuse them, but! You'd find surprising skeletal similarities.

Dolphins share a number of bones in common with humans, including the aforementioned finger bones. That's right. Their flippers contain a skeletal structure that looks like *a goddamn human hand.*[9]

Though we wouldn't confuse one animal with the next, the sharing of bones and structure is notable in the same way that stories—regardless of their genre or format or what-have-you—share bones and structure, too. A story works when a story works. No matter what the label is. No matter if it contains a masked killer or a space wizard or genetically modified dinosaurs. Of course different genres will have different tropes and particular expressions of these stories, in much the same way a dolphin has flippers and a blowhole versus a human's various bits and bobs. A story of any genre is going to contain elements of mystery, suspense/tension, drama, and conflict—even horror. A *lot* of non-horror stories contain bits of horror. Ever seen *E.T.*? Yeah, that's a nice sweet little movie about some bobble-head alien who gets stuck here on Earth and there's a

---

8   You'd at least need to put pants on the dolphin, and a dolphin cannot wear pants. Stop trying to put pants on dolphins. What is wrong with you?

9   Honestly, now that I typed that, it's freaking me out a little bit. What if dolphin fins are just gloves? And they take them off and have little creepy hands? Are dolphins people? Were they people? Were we dolphins? Will we become dolphins?? This is too much to worry about. This was supposed to be a nice book.

nice boy whose bike flies and there's the sweet little sister and then there's THE CREEPY MEN IN SUITS WHO COME TO STEAL E.T. AND OH NO E.T. IS TURNING GRAY LIKE MUSH AND HE'S REAL SICK OH GOD OUR PRECIOUS LITTLE ALIEN BOY IS DYING RIGHT IN FRONT OF US HOLY SHIT WHAT THE HELL.

The movie *When Harry Met Sally* ends *like a thriller*. It's New Year's Eve. Sally is about to leave the party she's at, alone and lonely and bored. Harry realizes he needs her and races in the cold to the party, and we think Sally is about to exit and he's going to miss her and that would be their shot to be together finally, after everything. He's running! There's a ticking clock! There's suspense that all could be lost! And even when they catch up to each other there's a tense exchange and it's not going well and we're on the edge as to whether or not these two crazy kids are going to figure it out and get to spend the rest of their lives together. And that's in a romantic comedy![10]

You have nothing stopping you from picking and choosing the elements you think will serve you and the story best. Pick whatever genre. Whatever trope. Whatever archetype. Whatever story elements. Grab them. Glue them together. Make them kiss. Make them fight.

In fiction, you can do literally *anything you want*.

So why wouldn't you?

---

10 Honestly, a lot of rom-coms have strong suspense/thriller vibes. The very nature of *will they won't they* is a form of tension baked into that romantic character dynamic. Which ultimately just goes to my point that genres are meant to be mashed together like narrative Silly Putty.

12

When Kids Ask Me for Writing Advice

BECAUSE I WROTE A MIDDLE-GRADE NOVEL, IT BECAME an expectation that I would do school visits and talk to children,[1] which I did. I visited my son's school and several other schools around the country (virtually, due to that pesky global pandemic, and now I'm worried that by the time you read this you'll instead be asking, "Which one?" because we'll be suffering from some virulent plague of goosepox or moon herpes), and during these visits I chose to ensure that the events accommodated time to have a robust Q&A session with the students.[2]

---

1 I know! They let me talk to children! I'm surprised, too, to be honest.

2 In part this is laziness. They always asked me, "What's your PowerPoint presentation going to be about?" And I was like, wait, what PowerPoint presentation? So instead I chose to just talk to the kids and then foist the rest of the time and work off on them, forcing the little goofballs to ask me questions. But this also worked because at my kid's own school, the teachers noted that the kids are often disappointed when they don't get to talk to the author, so that felt like a good thing to do, too. But mostly, laziness. Mmm. Sweet sweet laziness.

The kids of course would sometimes ask the weird questions one would expect of random children:

WHAT IS THE BEST STAR WARS CHARACTER AND WHY IS IT BOBA FETT?

HOW MUCH DOES THE HUMAN BUTT WEIGH AND ARE FARTS JUST GHOSTS?

WHO WOULD WIN IN A FIGHT, SPIDER-MAN OR OUR TEACHER, MISTER FENSTERMACHER?

All entirely fair questions.

But the surprising thing is, the kids also asked a plethora of really good questions about writing. Like, *hard* questions. I got questions about how you build suspense, how you make a character likable, how you know when to end a chapter or start a story. Real-deal questions! And further, I got questions that got to the heart of a writer's many dilemmas. Complicated *feeling* questions. Questions about inadequacy and of what to write, questions about how you know if a thing is any good or not, or why your story doesn't look like someone else's. You hear these questions and it's like, oh. *Oh.* You kid writers have the same questions we adult writers have. We never really grow up at all. We are haunted by the same doubts. Confused by the same processes. Unsure where to step at any moment.

Ultimately, a lot of the advice I give to them is the same advice I'd give to you, an adult.[3] But I think there's one piece I give to them which, upon further examination, is especially poignant for you, too, Adult Person, Presuming You're Not Just Three Children in a Trench Coat, and that advice is:

You need to have more fun in your writing.

---

3   Is there a kid version of "write drunk, edit sober?" "Writing is chocolate, editing is broccoli?"

Writing is a wild place. A carnival. A chaotic metaverse[4] where you are the divine programmer writing the code. We get caught up pursuing the results of our dreams rather than the dreams themselves: we walk on a path imagining first the destination and then the steps it will take to get there. We're a results-driven animal, a jumping spider plotting the erratic course to its prey, and there's certainly nothing wrong with that. But we've lost sight of the path beneath us, so focused on the horizon are we. In the case of writing, we're already imagining the publishing process. We're picturing the cover. What we'll do with the money.[5] How it'll earn us readers and fans. We hold the goal up so high, a bright, bold sun, that it washes out everything else that exists beneath it.

When I say "fun," I don't mean the story needs to *be* fun. I write a lot of very un-fun stories. But writers, I find, are occasionally monsters, and our version of fun can be quite twisted—as such, why not put that on the page? Whatever tickles that dark gland inside you, go for it.

Because there's more to writing than getting published.

We forget to play. We forget to *enjoy* ourselves.

We came to the page for a reason. We want to tell stories because it's fundamental to us, and it makes a certain sort of sense that we focus overmuch on the publishing part—because

---

4   True story, I wrote this bit and then only a few days later, Mark Zuckerberg announced that Facebook was rebranding as Meta and that the overall virtual experience of their product would be called the "metaverse." So if I get sued by that eyebrowless Plasticine android-from-the-Alien-universe, you know why. But honestly, if anybody should be suing anybody, Neal Stephenson should be suing him. Go read *Snow Crash*, won't you?

5   A WaveRunner, and endless meals of avocado toast. Like the billionaires do.

the publishing part is the part where it gets out there into the world, where the story *told* is a story *heard*, and that is ostensibly part of the drive to share stories in the first place. But we also get to relish the experience of a story and should also be able to relish the telling of one ourselves.

Mess around. Mess it up. Dance on the page. Fingerpaint clumsily. It's a canvas. A blob of clay. It's a sandbox, a bathtub, a wide-open expanse of possibility. Don't worry about what everyone else is doing. What you write won't look like that book you just read. It won't look like what the person sitting next to you is writing. And that's okay.

Dance on the page.

That's by design! We can't compare ourselves to other writers. Not only are they at a different point on the path, they're also different people entirely. Their path will never look like your path, and yours won't look like theirs. It's randomized. A rogue-like or rogue-lite dungeon crawl.

There's nothing wrong with writing a silly story.

Or a genre story.

Or a story about your life.

Or a story that is fan fiction, or that tries to sound like someone else's writing.

Or a story that is an experiment.

Or a story that makes no sense.

Or a story that has no end.

Or a story you write with one friend, or two, or three.[6]

---

6   I also told the students at school visits about how when I was in grade school, a group of friends and I had these big spiral notebooks we'd pass around. One of us would write a page, then pass it to the next person in rotation, and they'd continue the story—a madcap *Whisper Down the Lane* mode of storytelling. And the story was pretty batshit, featuring our own characters

Or a story based on some role-playing game you ran.

Or, or, or.

Any and all of it is okay.

And that's because you're just learning to do this thing. Nothing you do now will match a perfect vision inside your head, because the vision in your head is an outsized mirage. And worrying too much about publishing only limits what you can do here and now on the page.

Look it this way:

When you learn to walk as a baby, you do so because it's a delight, because it moves you around, because there's something intrinsically more *fun* about bobbling and tottering about instead of just sitting there on your bediapered bottom. You don't walk because you're already imagining your stint in the Olympics. When you play a game—a video game, a board game, or sports with friends—you aren't doing so because you imagine the Cash Prizes you're going to win, the Amazing Endorsements from Big Cool Companies you're going to nab.[7] You do it because it's fun. Because, *gasp*, you enjoy it.

Writers love to not enjoy their writing.

But maybe there's value in learning to love to write, too. Writing is work, and I've driven that home, but what if, and I'm just spitballing here—

---

but also characters from various pop-culture properties, and it was silly and occasionally crass and once in a while even sort of sweet. Part of the fun of it was that we learned how to entertain one another and surprise one another from page to page—how to build suspense, tell jokes, land character moments. It started off totally goofy but by the end of it, it became a real story.

7   To be fair, I don't think there are cash prizes or endorsements for board games yet. Though probably one day. SETTLERS OF CATAN WORLD CHAMPIONSHIPS, SPONSORED BY TACO BELL.

Writing was *play*, too?

What if sometimes you came to the page without a goal?

Without an expectation?

Without the pressure of what everyone else was doing?

What if the day's writing was just a pile of LEGO bricks? A tasting menu of foods you've never had? A forest with a trail you've never walked before?

What if it was okay to do whatever you wanted there? What if the page was the safest space of them all, a playground limited only by your own imagination?

What if writing was exploring? Map-making, wandering, adventuring?

What if—?

Maybe that's the best question of all.

Maybe that's the question that can drive you, if only today.

What if you did this?

What if you did that?

What if you did whatever made you happiest, or most amused, or most disturbed, or most delighted?

What if, indeed?

13

The Fine Art of
Flinging Fucks from
Your Fuckbasket

IT IS PERHAPS UNSURPRISING THAT PEOPLE ASK ME FOR
writing advice. Part of that is, obviously, I have long offered
dubious writing advice in various places,[1] and so people seek
me out at conferences or conventions or over email. Part of it is
just being a working professional writer. I write successfully,[2]
and therefore, people come to me, eyes wide, mouths agape, a
gentle-but-insistent panic flashing across their faces like distant lightning. And when they approach me seeking advice, a
lot of the advice they seek is not particularly specific. It can be,
for sure! Sometimes it's, "How do I create a compelling character arc," or, "How does one get through the gushy sloggy

---

[1]   Blog, books, yelling it at random citizens waiting for their bus to come.

[2]   Definition of which here is that I finish things and get them published.
I will say nothing of the quality of the work, for that is up to the readers to
decide. Also up to random Twitter accounts with egg avatars and eight dig-
its in their names who are definitely real people and not insane digital robots designed to make people's lives hell online.

middle of a book," or, "If I become a writer, do I have to wear pants, because I do not *do* pants?"[3]

But, just as often, and perhaps more than that, they approach with a kind of *wordless exhortation* of bewilderment and despair. Like they don't even know what to ask, or how—a sound forms less on their tongue and more on their breath, a kind of breezy *haaa whhhaa yyyyy uhhhh* emitting from their face-cave, maybe finally manifesting in a question like, "Wuzza wooza?" or "Nyhhhh?" or in the best-case scenario, "Me writer how?" They want to ask a question fully packed with all the questions, and the answer they want is an instruction manual, a Declaration of Wordependence, a road map, a crazy conspiracy wall with red yarn connecting the steps. Ultimately I think they mean, How do you do it? Like, how do you become a writer, how do you write as a writer, how do you *be* and *exist* as a writer, whether professionally or emotionally or just in the way that you're creating work that exists, that entertains, that *endures*. You scratch some paint off, and you find underneath it a writer who is paralyzed by all of this. By all the questions. By all the answers. By the bridge of uncertainty—a rope bridge, fraying and swaying in a hard, bullish wind—that connects both the Q's and the A's.

I don't generally answer their question in a way that is immediately satisfying, I fear. First, because, I got shit to do.[4] I can't yell my entire career into your face. Second, because my entire career is, like that of most writers, a desperate jump from a collapsing orbital station as I dive through jagged space debris in order to reenter the atmosphere and hurtle toward

---

3   Pants are a tool of the oppressor!

4   Like drink gin and stare into the void.

the ground, aided by gravity, while somehow, *somehow*, attempting to construct a, a, a helicopter or a wingsuit or a big inflatable hamster ball, anything that allows me to hit the ground and not immediately explode into a rain of viscera. Madness ensues! If you were to try to follow my career, duplicating each step accordingly, you would write five bad novels while both blogging to no one and also freelancing in the pen-and-paper game industry for a decade and in a moment of hitting bottom you'd write a novel you didn't know how to finish so you'd win a screenwriting competition that would both teach you how to write that unfinished novel and also take you eventually to the Sundance Screenwriters Lab, where the following year you'd have a short film debut at Sundance itself and then maybe just maybe you'd have that once-unfinished novel published by a small UK publisher.

Good luck. I'm sure you'll be fine!

Ahem. Yeah, no. You can't do what I did. And of course, you *shouldn't* do what I did. As painful as it is, you gotta do you, just as I had to do me.[5] You won't have to fall from the orbital station at all. You'll try to escape an exploding volcano full of lava bees, perhaps, or have to fight an elk.[6] Your chaos is yours to discover, to navigate, to survive. Just as every writer is a unique and individual entity, so is the journey of that writer.

But, see, here's the thing: at the end of the day, when I dig even deeper, I discover that this urgent despairing need to have *all the answers* to the one unutterable question of NYAAAAH

---

5   I don't mean "do me" in the sexy-time way, c'mon. What kind of book do you think this is, anyway?

6   A robot elk, and when you knock his head off, you realize it's your head underneath, because *you* were the robot elk all along.

HOW BE WRITER AM I DO? has ultimately nothing to do with actually needing those answers and seeking a map for this journey, and has everything to do with putting way, *way* too much pressure on yourself as a writer. So, when I feel that's the case, when I see the twitch in the plaintive writer's eye, when I see the panic dancing there in their gaze, I answer them in a way they don't expect, and in a way you may not expect now. And I answer them in a way that, at least initially, sounds like Very Bad Advice Indeed.

I say:

You need to learn to care less.

Now that sounds like Very Bad Advice Indeed because, obviously, pfft, pssh, you should only care *more*, right? If this thing you wanna do is a thing you really, really wanna do, then you cannot possibly care *enough*. It's all-the-chips-on-the-table time, time to bet everything.

Except, maybe not.

Maybe, just maybe, you're taking this *too* seriously.

Now bear with me—I'm not in *any way* suggesting that writing and storytelling and the making-of-art isn't vital. It's vital to the artist, and vital to the audience. Art matters. Stories change the world. Literally all of what we learn is told through some kind of narrative, through our understanding of art—even math and science are not disciplines that exist in a narrative vacuum. Mathematicians and scientists do what they do and learn what they learn to understand our world and solve problems—it's not just about data, but about the reasons we seek that data and the story that the data tells. *And* it's about writing that data down in a way that can be understood by an audience of other scientists and, potentially, more general audiences as well. History is made of stories. Religion is *made of* stories. Look no further than the golden ratio,[7] which is a mathematical relationship that ties together everything from medieval manuscripts to universal patterns found in nature to the architecture of Le Corbusier to the artwork of both da Vinci and Dalí. This stuff *is* important, even down to the stories we tell ourselves, the stories that move us to emotion and to action, to the artwork that changes our lives in ways both imperceptible and cataclysmic. And yet, my advice remains:

Learn to care less.

Why?

Consider our many autonomic processes.

Let's talk about three:

Breathing, walking, sleeping.

Do an experiment. Sit there, right now, and think about your breathing. In, out. In, out. Think harder about it. Are you doing it right? Are you breathing too fast, too slow? Are you getting enough oxygen in each breath? You might not be. What if you're not? In, out. In, in, out. Wait, did you do two *ins*? Is that normal? Are you okay? Are your lungs filling up enough? Too much? Are they working? Is your heart beating fast, too fast, too slow, is it even beating at all? Are you dead? Did you die? Are you a vampire ha ha you *fool* the ink on this page is distilled from allicin, one of the primary compounds of *garlic*, and I have poisoned you, foul night-beast, with the very ink of this book, a trick taught to me by my father, Charlie Van Helsing, mwa ha ha ha wait what's that? You're fine? Ah. Yes. See?

---

7   I promise I'm not high, but doesn't "the Golden Ratio" sound like a really delicious candy bar? I bet there's honey in it.

You're fine. Not a vampire at all. Breathing perfectly normally. Probably.

Extend this to walking. Ever think too hard about walking? God, I have. I remember being in junior high and thinking as I went down the hall, "Oh god, am I walking cool? Or am I walking in a really weird way? Am I even walking right? Is this correct? Are my hips supposed to do that? What is happening? Don't I know how to do this? Maybe I don't. *Oh god maybe I never did.*"

Or, try it during sleep tonight. Better yet, don't. Thinking too hard about sleeping—"Nnngh go to sleep now, okay, now, *now*, how about *now*, sleep sleep sleep what even *is* sleeping how do I reach the on/off switch sleeeeeep, you dipshit, *sleep*"— is a good way to make sure you don't ever sleep again.

So, if these very simple things we are quite used to doing become overly difficult under too much scrutiny and pressure . . .

Writing is not curing cancer. Well, how do you think writing is going to go with the same kind of intense observational anxiety? Not great, Bob!

Writing is not curing cancer.

You're not rescuing a baby from a well or saving a plane from crashing.

Could your story change the world? Save a life? Move mountains? Maybe. But is that why you're doing it? Is that why you come to the page every day? Or are you called to it because you like it? Because it's fun? Because your brain works that way and you're compelled to tell stories, or maybe just because you think you could be good at it? You can't control what the work does, or how important it becomes. You can only control what's there on the page.

And what's there on the page starts as a mess.

Certainly not always, and some days the words come with watchmaker's precision, but a lot of the time? *Hot-Ass Mess.*[8]

Writing feels like it should be a precise act . . . but it often isn't. Editing can be. Copyediting must be. Publishing is about as precise as catapulting pigs against the side of a building. End of the day, it's all kind of messy and weird.

Creative acts usually are.

And they benefit from that mess. They benefit from intellectual pipes unclogged by the sediment of worry. Too much pressure, those pipes will burst. The words must flow.[9] They flow when we feel allowed to do this, when we give ourselves permission, when we do not fear failure, when we absolve ourselves from the encumbrance of caring *too* much. That's how we make stuff. Just turning on the spigot and seeing what pours out. This will never really be automagic, like it is with breathing or sleeping, but you can get closer to it by, again, caring less.

> *The words must flow. They flow when we feel allowed to do this, when we give ourselves permission.*

---

8   If ever you doubted the importance of hyphen placement, look no further. HOT ASS-MESS is . . . well. It's not the image I'm going for, though if I'm being really honest with myself, some days, writing is that, too.

9   USUL, WE HAVE WORDSIGN THE LIKES OF WHICH EVEN GOD HAS NEVER SEEN.

However—

Note that I did not say stop caring at all. I can't have you reading this and assuming that the answer is you saying, "I don't give a fuck!" and then high-fiving yourself before kicking your laptop into a bucket of mopwater.

You have to keep some fucks in your fuckbasket. You must give *some* number of fucks to continue this thing that you want to do. It is important. It does matter. You matter in pursuit of it. You just can't keep *all* the fucks. All those fucks in your fuck-basket, they're too fucking heavy. There's too much *fuckdensity* going on there, which is definitely a scientific term probably. If you discard all your fucks and your fuckfields lie truly fallow, then nothing will grow there. But if you are too burdened by the weight of such fuckery, you won't be able to move; you'll remain paralyzed, neck-deep in fucks.

I only want you to lighten your load.[10]

You must have something in the tank to continue this pursuit.

But you can be bogged down by it, too.

And it's important not to get bogged down by the expectations *other people* put on you. Sometimes I tell people I'm a writer and they're like, "Do you win awards? Are you a bestseller? Do you know Stephen King?" As if those things are all the only metrics of value when it comes to being a writer.[11] As if it's not enough to have written a wonderful sentence today.

---

10 Sorry—"fuckload."

11 For the record, before editing this book I had won no awards but have since won the Dragon Award for Best Horror Novel, have been a bestseller though it took me some years, and I do not know Stephen King. I'm sure he's very nice though.

Sometimes that's all that matters. We run the risk of having others walk up to us and start depositing *fresh fucks* in our fuckbasket, weighing us down with *their* expectations, as if it's not jolly well goddamn enough that we overburden ourselves with our own expectations for ourselves. We don't need *your* judgment too, Aunt Becky.

The point is, chill out.

Release some of the pressure. Allow enough pressure to remain to push you forward, but vent the pressure that builds up and keeps you paralyzed in place.

(This is a tricky balance, admittedly; more on it in chapter 19.)

The goal is simply not to be crushed by the weight of your expectations. We set all these false mile-markers along our journey—*Well, I have to be published by the time I'm thirty, I have to win the Lord Fauntleroy Award for Literary Literariness, I have to finish this ten-book epic fantasy cycle about a throne made of dragons*[12]—but instead of markers for success, they're really just traps. Tripwires and oubliettes, the whole way. Free yourself from that. Care less. Don't stop caring altogether! We need you to care. The *story* needs you to care. But it needs you to care *just enough* to get it written. The rest is just a millstone hanging around your neck, innit?[13]

---

[12] But later you find out that all the DRAGONS are made of TINY THRONES. I'm giving away free ideas here, people. This stuff is gold. George R. R. Martin is feeling *pretty jellz* right now, as the kids say. Fleek and lit. Vibes. Yeah. I know the cool slang.

[13] I am now British.

14

The Joy of Fucking It All Up

PURITY AND PERFECTION ARE ENTANGLED TOGETHER.
When you approach the blank page, it's perfect. It's like your yard after snow: blanketed in white, untouched, unmarred, mounded soft hillocks and slow-swept waves of pillowy nothing. It's perfect because you didn't touch it. You left it alone and it remains, tabula rasa, an unwritten void. Because if you were to go out there onto that yard, what would happen? You'd get footprints all over it. You'd kick up those soft hills, those rounded curves. You'd dredge up a little mud, maybe some leaves left over from autumn. Sure, you'd make a snowman, and he's cool and all, but the area all around him is a scooped-up sloppy nightmare, because you needed to heave the snow to make the man. You'd bump into an evergreen branch and all the wonderful snow that had been elegantly sculpted upon it would go *choof* and fall down, and the waggle of the branch would move *other* branches too, and all *that* snow would come down in awkward plops and chonks, and you'd

scare away that astonishingly red cardinal[1] that was perched there. The page is like this, too. The moment you touch the blank page, you mess it all up. It's mucky with words, tacky with sentences. Some words might be misspelled. The grammar? Far from tip-top, if we're being honest. Was that opening line worth it? Are there too many commas? Not enough? Did you need that exclamation point? It was wonderful before you got here. Just the solace and the susurrus of the blank void.

That's how it feels to me, sometimes.

When I start to write—not every day, but literally whenever I go to start a new project—I feel this vertiginous feeling. Like I'm teetering on the edge of something, looking down through a cloud layer. Like I should just back up. Walk away. Give up. It's perfect now. Nothing I do will add anything. It will only subtract, I think. I'll punch my way down through the clouds, leaving a crass and ugly hole. I'll fall and flail. The white void will be interrupted, broken. It scares me. It literally scares me, staring at the blank page, the page before anything has been written—not a title, not a chapter header, not a first line. I get that tightness of going up a roller coaster, as you tick-tick-tick up toward the top, before the fall, before the screams and the wind and the oh-my-god-I'm-gonna-die.

Maybe you feel that, too.

Writing is scary.

It's okay.

Do it anyway.

Mess up the yard.

Leave footprints.

Jump off the cliff.

---

1   Bird, not religious figure.

Perfection is boring. It's dull. The weird snowman is what you want. The screaming and flailing, that's what you want, too. The mess, the mud, the muck, all of it. The words, the sentences, the bad grammar, the feelings, the fears. Reach out, step forward, fall down. It's okay. Stories aren't about perfection. Stories are messy. Authors are messy. So make a mess.

15

Nobody Knows What They're Doing

IF YOU FEEL LIKE YOU ARE THE ONLY ONE WHO DOESN'T know what they're doing and who has no idea what's going on, congratulations. You're just like me. And probably just like every other writer out there, with the exception of a few raging narcissists and solipsistic ego-pigs who are quite certain they are storytelling masters who know exactly what's going on.[1]

Nobody knows what they're doing.

Nobody knows what's going on.

Nobody knows anything.

Now, surely, someone out there is feeling their hackles rise a bit at this. Their teeth are buzzing with the need to correct me.[2]

I will clarify.

---

1   They aren't, and they don't.

2   The *Someone Is Wrong on the Internet!* impulse, made all the more difficult because you cannot yell at me in the book the way you can yell on social media. As a reasonable facsimile, feel free to highlight portions with which you disagree, and write your angry comments in as marginalia! What fun!

I am not saying that writers don't know how to write, or that publishing people don't know how to publish, or that editors and agents are unsure how to do all that *editing* and *agenting*. Publishing companies sometimes run massive focus groups. They may test for trends. Writers can spend years honing their craft, and editors spend the same time learning how to show writers how much more honing they've yet to do. Good agents develop relationships for miles and learn how to navigate the whirlpools and crushing rocks of this great publishing ocean.

In this, you might say, it becomes obvious that everyone knows very much what they're doing, thank you, and also, what the fuck. How dare *Chuck Wendig* slander[3] these very good people who very much know what they're doing.

Okay.

Yes.

But also—

No.

I know how to cook. I know how to bake. These are somewhat reliably routine processes. If I whisk a half teaspoon of cornstarch together with a half tablespoon of water, and then I further whisk in two eggs, plus a pinch of salt, I have begun the process of making kick-ass scrambled eggs.[4] If I warm a skillet over medium-high heat and melt another pat of butter in that skillet, then put the eggs into it, I can bully that egg mixture around the pan until it reaches the consistency I

---

3   Or is it libel? Slibel? Slibander? I dunno.

4   This trick, by the way, is thanks to Certified Food Genius J. Kenji López-Alt, who in turn learned it from food blogger Mandy Lee. Let me also tell you this trick works really well for omelettes.

desire. Upon releasing it from the pan, I know how it will taste. I know its texture. I can repeat this regularly, with little deviation from day to day. I know how to make scrambled eggs reliably, consistently.

Many of us know many things and can apply that knowledge reliably, reiterating to achieve something close to that consistency.

I know how to mow a lawn.

I know how to groom a horse.

I know to bake a loaf of sourdough bread.

Repeatable recipes.

Writing is not like this.

Publishing is not like this.

It is, perhaps, like this in a mechanical sense. I know how to, for instance, put one word after the next until it forms a sentence. I can put many sentences into a paragraph, and many paragraphs into a chapter, and on and on until a book is written. A publisher knows how to design a book, and copyedit it, and print and distribute it so that it reaches bookshelves. But that's pure mechanism. A book is not a product of only mechanism. A book is two covers with a whole lot of what-the-fuck sandwiched between them.

Earlier, I noted that I do not know how to write a book.

I also don't know how to write a book people will like.

Publishers don't know how to buy books people will like.

Editors do not know what developmental changes are *truly necessary* for a book to be objectively good.

> *There is no such thing as objectively good.*

That's because there is no such thing as objectively good.

And if there is no such thing as objectively good, then we have a very hard time repeating a creative process that ensures equivalent results every time.

Now this doesn't mean we aren't still experts, to some degree. The people in publishing—generally speaking—are experts in their fields. Many writers are very well practiced at what they do and have a strong grasp of what goes into telling a story. Booksellers and librarians are often *very, very good* at their jobs.

And yet—

None of them really *know* what they're doing. And by "know," I mean, "are 100 percent certain."

By which I mean they cannot predict what book will be an absolute bestseller. They are guessing. They're guessing in a way that is a guess born of great expertise, to be clear. It's not just punching in the dark. They are acting on a wealth of experience and listening to a chorus of their own intestinal flora that has long been cultivated by that experience. Just as many writers are listening to the same kind of *colonic wisdom* born of a well-trained, instinct-honed gut.

Consider:

An agent will represent an author and try to sell that author's book.

One editor may publish it, and the rest may reject it.[5]

Was that one editor right and the others all wrong?

Why, if everyone in publishing knows exactly what they're

---

5   And this is why it's vital for there to be more publishers and not, say, fewer publishers. A greater number of publishers means more opportunity for writers and for readers.

doing, would this not be fully repeatable? Why would they all not have made an offer?

What if the book is a rampaging success or a wretched failure? Is that an indictment against someone? Anyone? The system as a whole? The agent? The author? The booksellers who couldn't hand-sell it, the librarians who didn't know how to shelve it? The readers for not knowing Verifiable Genius when it has been shoved indelicately toward their eyeholes? If Margaret Atwood writes a book, why isn't it as successful as her most successful book? Or even close? If everyone knows what they're doing, why isn't every book a bestseller?

Because nobody really knows what they're doing.

We're all just guessing.

This is not only okay, but it's essential.

First, because that's part of the fun. Who wants uniformity and certainty in writing? This is a creative, pyroclastic realm. It's not IKEA furniture.

Second, because if nobody knows what they're doing, then you can feel free to ignore every guru proclamation about what you absolutely must write. This trope, that trend, these genres—nobody knows what really works or what's truly going to land well in twelve to twenty-four months, so you can instead just say *fuck it* and write whatever thing that lives in your heart.

Third, because now you don't have to feel so bad. You feel like you don't know what you're doing? You're right. You don't. Not truly, not completely, not in a way that is repeatable and reliable. And nobody else knows either. You're not alone in this. You are in a sea of equally lost and bewildered souls who are just trying to figure out how to make cool art and find their place in a chaotic universe.

It's okay not to know what you're doing. You don't have to know with absolute certainty what will work. Art and stories don't really want to be pinned down that way, anyway. If we all had some shared common understanding that $1 + 1 = 2$ in storytelling, everybody would do it, and the whole beast would lose its teeth. Art does not want to be domesticated.[6] Let it be wild and uncertain.

---

6   Worth offering a counterpoint here that your publisher should not throw up their hands and say, "Nobody knows anything, huzzah!" They still must bring their expertise (and ideally, money) to bear on publishing your book. Getting hit by lightning isn't easy, but there are ways to make it easier, such as running out into a storm with a lightning rod tied to your head. It's the publisher's job to identify the storm and hand you a lightning rod.

16

When Is It Good to Feel Bad? A Helpful Guide!

WE WRITER-TYPES TEND TO LIVE INSIDE OUR HEADS.

Obviously, we live outside our skulls, too—the world in which we live is a vital resource for what goes on the page, an ever-refreshing spring of water from which to drink. Even still, what goes on *out there* *gesticulates wildly* still ends up landing *in here* *taps forehead* before it gets all tumbled around, scrambled up, whipped into a froth, and shellacked onto the page.

Our lives are often quite internal.

This can be occasionally fraught.

And that's because the insides-of-our-heads can be a dangerous place. There are booby traps all over. Wolves hunt in that place. There are *LEGO bricks* scattered *everywhere* and mentally speaking you are wearing neither *shoes* nor *socks*.

So this internal process runs into the perils and pitfalls native to that mental and emotional realm. It's like playing Dungeons & Dragons—if you want the treasure, you gotta fight the beholder.[1] The good shit is in the dungeon, or under the dragon's belly. Something-something no-risk no-reward blah blah blah.

And for a long time, some of my advice—ultimately to myself, and maybe to you if it's useful—was there to help defeat a lot of the brain goblins that besiege our creative castles. Like, boom, here's how you kick your self-doubt in the face! Here's how to karate Impostor Syndrome in the crotch! Here's how to detonate the whale of writer's block with a crate of TNT so that its blubbery guts will rain down upon the town in a torrent of scalding viscera!

But, as with all things, I am constantly refining my process and also constantly refining how I think about my process—and, in fact, how I think about all of the gnarly, fiddly bits of the craft, the art, and one's overall life of writing.

And I'm coming around to thinking that these negative bits—maybe they're not so bad. They can be, of course, and we'll talk about how to see that more clearly. But I think it's important to see that these negative thoughts and feelings are

---

1   Here is where I note the embarrassing detail that for a not-unreasonable part of my life, I just assumed the phrase, "Beauty is in the eye of the beholder" meant that beauty was in the eye of the actual monster known as the Beholder. That didn't make the phrase particularly cogent, but then again, half the time old sayings and platitudes don't make a lick of goddamn sense anyway. "Have your cake and eat it too," well, what the hell does that mean? I can have cake, and then eat some of that cake, and still possess cake. That is literally the nature of cake. "Don't look a gift horse in the mouth." Well, why not? It's my horse, apparently. Also why are you giving me a horse? I didn't ask for that. Now I'm going to have to buy Horse Chow and that shit is expensive, so honestly the horse is barely a gift, more of a curse. So you bet I'm going to look in its damn mouth. What were we talking about again?

entirely normal. That they're a part of it. And if they're a part of it, if they're normal, then maybe they bring *some* value to the table at *some* level. Maybe they're doing something for you, and it behooves us as writers to figure out just what that "some-

> *These negative thoughts and feelings are entirely normal.*

thing" happens to be. If they're organic to the process, if they belong to us, then we have to figure out why. And we have to embrace them, bumps and gnarls and knots and all.

"Vulpine" Is a Cool Word and You Know It

That, then, is our first task.

It's to figure out the answer to this question:

When is a bad thing truly a bad thing?

When is it part of us, and when isn't it?

In that, I speak to you of *foxes*.

Those who follow me on social media[2] may be aware that once upon a time, my writer's shed was beset on all sides by foxes. One day, I saw two foxes in the woods, and a few days later, I saw a third fox—this one much smaller, either a minia-turized fox or, more likely, a fox baby.[3] And then, in the days ensuing, more of them emerged, to the point that I realized there were four or five such *baby foxes* running around. They were lovely. Their den was literally about ten feet behind my

---

2   Dear god, why?

3   Aka, fox kits, fox pups, widdle-bitty foxy friends.

writer's shed, and as time went on, they would play out front of the aforementioned shed while I was in there writing. Several times they actually *came to the door*, pawing at it, as if asking to be let in.[4]

We watched them every day.

We watched them learn to do the much-vaunted *mouse-pounce*, where they leap up in the air, their lithe bodies forming a parabolic arc before crashing back down on the location of a presumed mouse. They did this with dog toys we'd left in the backyard. They also did this with . . .

Well, baby bunnies.

Cute, wonderful, adorable little floof-ball baby bunnies.

The foxes would leap.

They would catch a little bunny.

Then they would play with it for a while before eating it.

Baby bunnies.

Baby bunnies.

And here, then, is the point:

That sounds bad. And, for the bunnies . . . ennnh okay yeah it's pretty bad. But, at the same time, the baby foxes have to eat. They also have to learn to hunt. And the universe will continue to make more baby bunnies. It's literally part of that whole *rabbit* metaphor—rabbits breed like, well, rabbits. It is terrible and sad that the foxes eat them, but, not to get all

---

4   Please believe me, if ever you doubt my willpower, know it is real and it is like steel, for that day I *did not open the door*. The foxes called me to adventure and I did not answer that call, for fear of naturalizing the foxes to the comfort and safety of humans. Humans are monsters, and I needed them to be afraid of me, or at the very least, totally uninterested. But don't think I to this day regret not finding out where the fox adventure would have taken me. I bet it would've been great.

Mufasa on you, that's the circle of life, Simba. Meaning, it's part of things. It is nature red in tooth and claw. And while it may seem sad, too many rabbits would itself cause a kind of imbalance, wouldn't it? In fact, in places where we remove vital predators from the ecosystem, we see an increase in ticks, in disease, in crops and other plants being eaten—there are negative ramifications to that, a ripple effect. Reintroducing wolves to an area, for instance, tends to revitalize that ecosystem—you see burgeoning populations of prey animals, bolstered riparian areas, and more wildflowers growing. And you think, wait, what, more wildflowers? Are wolves planting flowers?[5] No. But deer and elk, without predators to harry them, tend to stay in one place, trampling the ground, stopping plants from growing there. And rabbits will eat whatever grows. But if wolves are there to move the herds, like hungry shepherds, then the ground is less trampled, and more plants grow because more plants go uneaten. Wildflowers sprout. And wildflowers bring pollinators like bees and butterflies, and birds follow, because they want to eat those pollinators or because they want the seeds that the wildflowers make. Reintroduce wolves, and you get more songbirds and wildflowers. More beauty in the world.

Weird, but true.

And that's despite seeing wolves as hungry predators causing suffering—which, to be clear, is a very anthropomorphic notion, this idea that somehow their hunting and killing of other animals is wrong, unnatural, sinful.

But, of course, it's not always that way, is it?

Wolves help the areas to which they are *native*.

---

5   Yes. Okay, no. But I like the image, so yes.

But some creatures and some plants are not native at all. They are invasive.

Marmorated stinkbugs, lanternflies, bindweed, snakehead fish, and so forth. As creatures, it's not their fault. But if they are not indigenous to an area, they come in, find no competition for resources because nothing there knows how to kill or eat them, and they thrive. Which means pushing out native species. Which throws the ecosystem out of balance, and then . . . fewer wildflowers, fewer songbirds. Nature, out of whack.

And so that, to me, is the test.

The negative things you experience as a writer—the self-doubt, the Impostor Syndrome, the rejection, the failure—could be like the fox, or the wolf. They might be essential to you. They might be essential to the work. Or they might be like bindweed: crawling all up in your dirt, pushing everything good *out*.

The real test is:

Are they helping you continue your process?

Or are they stopping it in its tracks?

Are the bad feelings you feel and the negative effects normal? Are they, for lack of a better term, native to the experience? Or are they invasive to it?

How, exactly, do you tell?

Let Us Speak of Self-Doubt

Self-doubt. It's a big issue, I think. Maybe *the* big issue for writers.

We all have it. My son has it when he goes to write something. You probably have it when you write. I have it when I write now. When I write anything! My last book, the one before that, all the books that came and all the ones that are, I hope, yet to arrive. Hell, I'm feeling it *right now.*

Maybe I'm not good enough. Maybe this book isn't good enough. Maybe this sentence could be better.

And I think, you know, if we're all experiencing it, and many of us are experiencing it on the regular . . .

Then it's normal.

And if it's normal . . .

Then at the best, it is of value, and at the worst, we can ignore it.

The value might be that it tests us, a little bit. The very act of editing is an act of accepting and embracing self-doubt, isn't it? It's an acknowledgment of imperfection. It's saying, "Hey, I know this isn't quite right. I *doubt* that the work, and myself as a writer, reached the level the story needs to reach." But it's also saying, "Okay, so what does that mean? How do I proceed, and how do I fix it?" While acknowledging error and doubt, it's also giving purpose to that doubt—it's saying that there is a way forward. There is *a fix.*

Imagine if you didn't have self-doubt at all. You'd just bolt forward, certain in your awesomeness. Like a narcissistic lightning bolt! You'd accept the critical touch of no agent, no editor. You might become one of those mythical authors whose books are Too Important to Edit, Too Big to Fail. Except you might never reach that mythical height in the first place because you'd never have been edited, never have edited yourself, never have accepted the wanton imperfections native to the work and to yourself.

Accepting imperfections is powerful.

It is essential.

As is accepting that though you may never make yourself

Though you may never make yourself or the story perfect, you can always improve.

or the story perfect, you can always improve. You are a blade that can be sharpened. Every story can be made stronger.

That's *huge*.

And if the self-doubt isn't doing that for you, then it's easy enough to discard. Because sometimes the normalcy of it is just that it comes like rain—it's a fact of life, a part of the cycle, and maybe you need to just wait it out. Maybe the problem isn't self-doubt, but rather, letting that doubt control you.

You Don't Belong Here

Self-doubt opens the door, and Impostor Syndrome walks in.

As always, we must define our terms, and Impostor Syndrome is this: you feel like a fraud. You feel like you don't belong. Every day can feel like your first day at a new job: someone shoved a clipboard in your hand, slapped a hard hat on your fool head, then asked you to perform a task you don't understand using words you've never heard before. Every mental klaxon in your brain is going I DON'T KNOW WHAT THE FUCK I'M DOING followed by OH GOD EVERYONE IS STARING AT ME THEY KNOW I CAN'T DO THIS.

It feels, y'know, *not great*. I don't know that every writer experiences it—but I know I do, and again, I'm an author sitting on a not-unreasonable nest egg of finished, published books. And even there, sitting upon that heap of actually actual books, I still think, "They're going to catch me." Like one day all my readers and all my fellow writers and the entirety of the publishing industry are going to turn toward me, silently, in unison, realizing collectively that my books have just been erratic sketches of cats looking over their cat shoulders as they show you their cat buttholes. [Editor: please insert hastily drawn sketch of cat blankly regarding its own butthole here.][6] And at that, they'll vote me off Author Island.

But I've come to really, really love that feeling.

To switch gears for a moment, if you have a child, or you are yourself a twelve-year-old mentally,[7] you are aware of a game called Among Us. In this cartoon-style multiplayer game, you play these round, egg-shaped astronauts just bobbling around your ship or space station, doing the menial tasks necessary to keep yourself anchored to the void of space. But one of the players is not an astronaut, though their character still looks like one: that player is controlling an *impostor*.

The impostor is an alien monster hiding in plain sight.

You look like them.

But you aren't them.

Your job, in fact, is to *pretend to be them* well enough that you can sneak around the ship and murder them one by one, picking off the unsuspecting astronaut ding-dongs and doing so with enough tricksy aplomb so that they don't vote you off the ship. In fact, the power move is to execute the other characters in a way that makes them think *one of their own* is actually the impostor—in which case they throw some poor innocent fool out of the airlock, where they die in space.

---

6   They didn't insert one, did they. Goddammit.

7   As I most certainly am, evidenced by the fact I think "cat-butthole sketch" is funny.

And meanwhile, you get to keep on killin' these space dopes.

It's silly. It's fun. A toony app version of John Carpenter's *The Thing*.

The impostor is the best role in the game.

Just as the impostor is the best way to view yourself as a writer.

The impostor is the best way to view yourself as a writer.

Here's why.

First, it is both fun and freeing to admit you don't know what you're doing while trying to pretend that you absolutely *do* know what you're doing.[8]

Second, you soon come to realize that *every* writer is an impostor. Writing is an outsider's job. It's who we are and what we do—we sit outside the light, in the dark, watching everyone else. We don't belong, which is why we're *writers*. We're strangers, observers, recorders and reporters of the odd, the unusual, the edge-case weirdness. So if you're an impostor? You're in the right place. We're a garage full of feral cats, but none of us is part of the colony, you feel me?

Third and finally, just like in *Among Us*, you are a monster cloaked in human flesh who will hunt the unsuspecting meatbags! They'll never catch you! Ha ha ha! Mwa ha ha! Uhh, I mean, I'm just kidding. Obviously. *Obviously.*[9]

Point is, it's normal to feel like a fraud, to feel like you don't

---

8   And by the way, this is how you end up knowing what you're doing. Fake it till you make it is sometimes bad advice, and I wouldn't recommend it if you worked at a hospital or a nuclear reactor. But in writing, nyeaaaah, it mostly works.

9   Super sus.

belong, like you're a stowaway on this ship, like you're an uninvited guest to this party.

But real talk, being the stowaway, or the party-crasher, is an awesome job. You snuck on board. You're in a mask. They haven't caught you yet. *Triumph.*

The F-Word

Of course, even embracing the notion that you might be a fraud, there is another f-word that stirs tumult in the heart of the writer:

Failure.

And this one is a big one.

Failure is the doom-word, the killing breath. It's the knife in the heart, the one that goes all the way through the chest and out the back.

We have long held the wrong ideas about failure.

But I'll posit that we have long held the wrong ideas about failure. It starts in school (as so many bad memetic trends often do), where when we *fail* something, it is summarily viewed as the *worst thing that can happen*. You failed! F-minus! You suck!

And yet, failure is an essential part of all our processes.

Getting good at something first requires being bad at that particular something.[10] I wrote five books before getting one published. Those books were all ostensibly failures. I failed to

---

10 Okay, this isn't universal—some people try a thing and nail it on the first attempt. Those people are called robots and we should be wary of them because one day they will harvest our brains for their MEAT COMPUTERS.

finish many more books before and during those five books, and *those* books were even bigger failures. I've had published books land on bookshelves with little more than an unceremonial *flushing* sound. Were those books failures? Probably, at least by some metric—yes, they were published, yes, I was paid, but no, they didn't ever earn out.[11] If this were school, I'd be a forty-year-old man sent back to kindergarten, greedily eating paste out of my hand.

But this is reality, and all those failures were *completely useful and necessary.* I only got to where I am now by making and enduring those failed attempts. It sounds counterintuitive to suggest that success comes through failure, but it does. Failure is the tunnel we all have to go through. And it's not a one-and-done thing either. I've failed before and will fail again. Hell, maybe *this very book* will fail. Maybe no one will read it: a tomb of words overgrown by ivy.

> *Failure is the tunnel we all have to go through.*

Failure is magic. It's an instruction manual written in scar tissue. It's a heap of garbage we made that we can use to climb to greater heights. "Oh, did I break all this stuff and leave ruinous debris everywhere? Onward and upward!" Failure is amazing. Fail more. Fail often. Fail big and weird. The trick is just trying to learn something from it—the aforementioned *instruction manual* part. Just as we should read and write with mindful intent, so too should we fail mindfully.

---

11   "Earning out" is the process by which your book sales grow beyond the advance you were paid, meaning once you surpass this advance, you begin to collect royalties. This entire process is governed by a trio of witches, a magical possum, a haunted sextant, and a sentient spreadsheet that lives in the sewers of New York City.

Failing is like falling. We need to learn how to do it. We need to learn how to fall and not shatter ourselves into a million little pieces—and we need to fall to learn how to pick ourselves back up again and keep going. From the earliest point of walking, that is literally why we fall. Walking is itself an act of falling, isn't it? Putting a foot out and falling forward, knowing that you'll catch yourself and move forward. Failing is falling, and both are essential.

Battle Scars and Armor Dents

Your failure might be born of rejection.

It has been for me in the past. Rejection is certainly more of a *publishing* problem than a *writing* one, but it's notable just the same, assuming that traditionally publishing the work is part of your path.[12]

Consider: I've had short story rejections, too many to count.

Those five trunk novels of mine? All rejected at some point by an agent.

My first original novel, *Blackbirds*? Yes, it got me an agent, but after that, it was rejected for almost *two years* by every major publisher, and the rejections there were additionally confusing—so many rejections were of this flavor: *Why yes, we love this book very much! We love it so much we apparently can't publish it because our sales teams don't know how to sell it. No, no,*

12　And even in indie/self-publishing, you end up suffering rejection at the hand of reviewers and customers. Any bad review is a rejection. Any time someone chose not to click *buy*, that's a rejection.

we don't want you to change it! If you changed it, it wouldn't be the book we loved, now would it? And yet, as is, we cannot publish it. Good luck! It was only at the end of that process that we found two smaller overseas publishers willing to duke it out a little bit for rights to publish the book.

And even now, my books get rejected. Even when they succeed, they still go through a gauntlet of rejection. To get to one *yes*, you have to go through an unholy tornado of *no*. A no from damn near every publisher! Even when you win, you lose. Because that's publishing.[13]

Rejections are the water in which we swim. They are normal. They are part of it. They're like battle scars or dents in your armor: proof that you've been in the fight, scrapping for your book and your career. The thing to remember most is that this failure isn't really in your hands. Rejections aren't personal, and more importantly, they're not even objective. How could they be? Someone somewhere is guessing that your book is going to be the right book to sell—or not, as it were—based on imperfect evidence. Even if your book appears to be on trend, by the time that book lands on shelves, that trend might be long in the grave. At the end of the day, an offer or a rejection is based on people's feelings—the feeling that the book is not necessarily *good* but that it will be *right,* and further,

Rejections aren't personal, and more importantly, they're not even objective.

---

13 Separate from this, a little bit, is how Traditional Publishing differs from the Film and TV business. In New York Publishing, everything is *no* before it's *yes*. But in Hollywood, everything is *yes* before it's *no*.

that it will in some way become *profitable*. That's not personal. It's purely subjective. It's a guess. A hope. A dream shared collectively with a potential publisher.

Winners Never Quit, Quitters Never Win, and Other Such Fuckery

Rejection may want to make you quit.

And once again, we must evaluate a theoretically bad thing through the lens of *But is there something good about it, though?*

I've long railed against writers quitting.

DO NOT QUIT, I would bellow and yawp. Frothing and shaking my fist. FAILURE IS OKAY, BUT QUITTING IS NOT. Never give up! Never surrender![14]

But.

Buuuuuut.

I look back over my writing and my career and . . .

Wow, quitting has been very useful sometimes.

I've done it a whole lot! All the time! I quit stuff like a *proud quitter*, a professionally trained, bonded, licensed, and insured *resigner-of-things*.

I've started and bailed on dozens—*dozens*—of novels. They are little more than hacked-in-half story corpses, as if I am a serial killer of potential novels, slicing them in bloody twain before they ever get to live a full life.

I've quit writing gigs and jobs that didn't feel right—either

---

14   It just occurred to me that this phrase, from *Galaxy Quest*, is redundant. Those things mean the same thing! Which is probably the point but I'm just figuring it out now, shut up.

didn't feel right for me at that time or that felt in some way exploitative or problematic.

Consider: In 2021, I had two novels out, *The Book of Accidents* and *Dust & Grim*, the former an adult horror novel, the latter a middle-grade spoopy horror-fantasy. The two books have quite a bit in common: set in Pennsylvania, each dealing with the trials and tribulations of family, both having to do with the executorship of an estate upon death. But one curious thing that they have in common I haven't talked much about? Each was a book I'd tried to write before.

Book of Accidents I tried writing twice, once about ten years ago, another about twenty. The first attempt I had finished, but it wasn't good. The second attempt I didn't even finish. *Dust & Grim* was a book I tried writing in . . . I think 2013, and it didn't feel right, so I got about halfway through it and bailed on it. In both cases I failed those books, and in both cases, I quit on them, too.

And it was only now, years later, that I found the right way to tell those stories. They weren't the wrong books. I was the wrong writer for them at the time. I needed . . . life, context, experience, some *ineffable spark* to succeed with them. But quitting on them was the best thing I could've done.

Quitting on them was how they were born.

Sometimes, quitting isn't taking a step back, it's going forward. It's like being stuck in traffic and deciding to go off onto a side street—yes, you've quit the path you were on, but you found another way, a side way. And

> *Sometimes, quitting isn't taking a step back, it's going forward.*

even if that way is less efficient, it still gets you there. Or maybe you end up somewhere else entirely, and while in life that's often not ideal . . . in writing, it is often *very* ideal indeed.

I think the only form of quitting that's more worrisome is the kind where you close the door and never again open it. But even there—who's to say that's wrong? This sounds almost profane to say, but there does come a point when realizing a thing isn't for you is an unvarnished, unalloyed good. I once wanted to be a cartoonist, and while it feels sad to say I quit on that dream, I also think, well, it's damn good I did, because if I hadn't, maybe I wouldn't be who I am today. I wouldn't be *here* if I were *there*, which is a thing that seems very obvious when you say it out loud, but that doesn't make it any less difficult to truly enact and grasp, does it? If you're not a writer, then you're not a writer. The sunk cost fallacy is a fallacy for a reason: we have a tendency to think we will lose time and effort on a thing, and by investing that and *continuing* to invest that, we can somehow regain it. But lost is lost. You can't get it back. You can't throw stuff into a bottomless hole in the hopes of filling it up. So, if your writing path ends with you deciding, *nope, not for me*, that's okay. In fact, it's amazing to realize that, to be free of something. Please understand, this isn't me encouraging all of you to quit. I've felt like quitting a hundred times, a thousand times, and I didn't, and I'm glad for it. But also . . . I am encouraging you to do it, if that's the right thing for you. Because at the end of the day, here's the wondrous thing about quitting writing: you can un-quit. It's not a contract with the universe. You didn't *sign* anything. You just say, today, you're not a writer. Don't like it. Don't wanna do it anymore. Good riddance and goodbye.

And if that feels right a year later, excellent.

And if a year after that you think, *Hey wait, maybe I do wanna do this . . .*

Then you go and do it again.

Quitting is temporary, if you need it to be.

I think we should quit more things, honestly.

Blocked and Reported

And then—

Flash of lightning.

There's the big one.

Crash of thunder.

The doozy.

The one we are most often asked about.

The one we most often talk about.

And fret about.

And suffer from.

A wolf howls in the distance.

WRITER'S BLOCK.

The earth trembles.

I'm not kidding when I say it's one of the most frequent things I'm asked about.[15] When I talked to schools about my middle-grade novel *Dust & Grim*, it was one of the things that came up every time.

---

15   Well, almost as frequently as, "Sir, why are you standing in the shrubbery dressed like a clown, holding a camping hatchet in one hand and a barn owl in the other?" To which my answer is inevitably, IT IS PART OF MY PROCESS, LEAVE ME ALONE, YOU CANNOT CENSOR ME.

That's right! The question even plagues *children*. It's like Freddy Krueger, writer's block. Stalking us in our nightmares from the earliest age.[16]

So, first and foremost, we're going to talk about writer's block—what it is, where it comes from, how to deal with it. But we're also going to talk about why it's not necessarily a bad thing. (That is, after all, the thesis here: that not all the bad vibes that plague us writer-types are necessarily problems.)

Writer's block is what it says on the can: you, the writer, are somehow blocked from continuing to write. Usually it's specific to the thing you're writing, but it can also be a more generic, generalized block—*I can't push forward on anything* rather than *I can't push forward on this particular story*.

And here is where it is very, very important to note that sometimes . . .

Writer's block is *not* writer's block.

Writer's block might instead be a mental illness masquerading as writer's block, like some kind of Scooby-Doo villain.[17]

Now, before you clench up too tight, let me *also* say that though the phrase "mental illness" has negative connotations, please believe me when I say I do not mean it pejoratively—I myself am the host of, at bare minimum, a rock-solid case of generalized anxiety disorder. Mental illness is profoundly common and should have no more judgment attached to it than,

---

16   One wonders when we will receive proof on a cave wall that Neanderthals experienced writer's block. HROG NOT DRAW MAMMOTH CARTOON TODAY. HROG NOT FEELING CONFIDENT ABOUT DIRECTION OF STORY. HROG SAD.

17   Zoinks!

say, having to wear glasses for reduced eyesight, or having mi-
graines, or suffering from arthritis. Our brains are complex
thinky-machines and in that complexity lurks various vulnerabilities, and these illnesses and neurodivergences are a profound part of us. And I suspect that artists and storytellers are
just as likely, if not more so, to host such non-neurotypical
brain gremlins.

Furthermore, since I am apparently nothing if not *a man
made of caveats*, let it also be stated boldly that I am not a certified brainologist. I am not a person trained in any way, shape,
or form on the subject of these mental illnesses. I only know
what I deal with, and how I deal with it, and that's as far as I
can take it, because I'm not you. Okay? Okay.

So, with all that being said, writer's block is sometimes
anxiety and depression masquerading as writer's block, or
OCD or adult ADHD, it seems. The point I want to make is
that you cannot address these things in the way you would address actual writer's block. You can't just "write your way
through" depression, for example. It's like trying to climb out
of quicksand—all that thrashing about will only make you
sink deeper.[18] You can't "find the plot problem" in anxiety.

How can you tell if your writer's block is the real thing or
whether it is just your brain doing its strange brain things? I
don't know that there's a really good, proper way to check—you
can't simply dip a hot copper wire in a dish full of blood to test
for it. But I think there are some clues. I think writer's block is
often based in the work, and I think the writer's brain is eager
to solve it inside the work, but I think if it's anxiety or

---

18 Plus, all that moving around summons *quicksand sharks*. Didn't know
about those, did you?

depression, it tends to be more persistent, and your enthusiasm to solve the problem may feel either dampened or additionally frustrating. It may be that you don't want to write *anything*, and if your writer's block is a generalized catch-all demotivational vibe, it might not be writer's block at all. Speaking for myself, when anxiety is manifesting as writer's block, I tend to feel panicked, like the whole thing is impossible. And friends with depression describe it as feeling like the writing is in a dead zone—an inaccessible place. Again, such illnesses do not in any way indicate that you are broken, and they are a regrettably normal part of our lives. They're just not writer's block, and you can't solve one as if it's the other.[19]

So! Let's say you have *actual real-deal writer's block*.

Then what?

First, you recognize that it is normal and it is real. There are writers who will tell you that *writer's block does not exist*, or the version I've occasionally said, which is, *I do not personally experience writer's block*. This is a lie. It's not a willful deception, it's just that the writer's block they (and I) have experienced has felt so normal they don't qualify it with the title, but trust me: every writer experiences it in some way. Any day where you feel frustrated with the writing, or uncertain where to go next? Yeah, uh, that's writer's block. And it's important to realize that *non*-writers experience it, too, except it's not writer's block, it's just, y'know, plumber's block,[20] or mathematician's

---

19 And here I note that if you do have a mental illness with which to grapple, you are best consulting a mental health professional and not, say, me. I certainly don't have *my* shit together half the time, so I should not be trusted to help button yours up, either.

20 Hey, that's actually kind of a pun. Because, y'know, plumbers deal with blockages. Blocked pipes. So, plumber's block. Get it? Ahem.

block, or kid's party clown block. Hell, I get it as a parent. Sometimes your kid flummoxes you in such a way you're like, "I don't know how to deal with this problem and I need to go lie down, please remain in this place, child-of-mine, until the time comes when I emerge from my nap-cocoon to render some kind of judgment."

Second, you need to take some time to try different things out. What you do with that time is particular to you and the work at hand. Every writer and every story is different, and it's one of the reasons that writing a lot and iterating that work mindfully helps bring you more clarity on this than I can likely deliver here. Maybe step away from the story for a day or two. Or go take a walk, mow the lawn, have a shower—anything that moves the blood around, because blood carries necessary oxygen to your brain. You may instead find that your block is specific to the story at hand, and that might mean you need to go back and look at earlier portions of the work to see if you took a wrong turn.[21] Perhaps you're simply bored with the work and need to find a way to regain the excitement—juicing it up with a surprise, an explosion, a betrayal, a twist, anything to keep you interested.[22] Maybe a character isn't working. Or a plot point feels contrived. It requires a bit of narrative detective work, is all.

And therein lies the secret:

Writer's block isn't all bad.

---

21 Storytelling is sometimes like doing a maze on the back of a cereal box. You're going to hit a dead end and that means going back to find a better way to go.

22 And of course the value of keeping yourself interested means your readers are likelier to remain interested as well. Surprising yourself means surprising them.

Because, if you really think about it, writer's block is sometimes like a warning light letting you know *something is off*. It is a tremor in the spider's web, or an ill wind blowing. It's doing us a service, as bad as it might feel. Think of writer's block as the voice of your *intestinal flora*, the choir of hypersentient bacteria in your gut that provides the insight of *instinct*. You can ignore them and push on—that's okay, too, long as you fix in edit—and there's also nothing to say our instincts are universally correct. But for my mileage, any time I begin to slow down on a work and start to want to hit the brakes, feeling that writer's block vibe, it's usually a sign from my subconscious

> *Writer's block is sometimes like a warning light letting you know* something is off.

that it's time to rethink some things. It is indeed time to take a walk and noodle a great many thinky-thoughts about the work, to perform a lot of narrative cross-checks and internal character diagnostics to make sure everything feels like it's hanging together properly.

It's also fine and good to persevere and push on. My process in this regard needn't be your process: certainly there's value to mashing the accelerator and driving that machine as fast as you can till the thing either gets you over the finish line or explodes in a fiery ball before tumbling down a plot hole big enough to swallow Central Park. You can always fix it in subsequent drafts. The point stands, though, that writer's block isn't necessarily all bad. There's gold in them thar hills.

The question is whether you can dig for it.

What Belongs, and What Doesn't

Once more, I return to the notion of *native* versus *invasive*.

And I asked earlier how you tell?

Again, as with so much of this, there's no real test to be had, but one thing I know is that we are often poisoned by other people's negative thinking. Sometimes people tell us a thing, a bad thing, a doubtful thing, a derogatory thing, and it enters our head. For a time we know it's their voice, not ours, but once it's in, we start to ask the question, *But what if they're right?* What if they're right that I'll never make it, that I shouldn't waste my time on this, that I'm not good enough? And eventually, that voice echoes around our brain cave so often and so deeply that the echo returns to us, and it's no longer in their voice—

It's in ours.

It's like they plant terrible seeds in us, and they sprout awful trees.

There's value in realizing that you didn't plant those trees. They did. These poison thoughts are not your own. Feel free to spite these thoughts and those who planted them in your head.

Spite will get you there. Spite will lead you to create. The desire to prove that damning echo wrong, that's spite. And sometimes we create work in spite of them, or even *to* spite them. And there's no harm in that, either. Whatever gets you to the page. Whatever gets you to write. We are under siege from negativity and bad thoughts, but they're not always there to hurt us. Sometimes we can make use of them. Sometimes they show us things about ourselves. And when they don't? When they don't belong? We realize we can kick them aside and keep moving.

Something Important, Part Five

IT'S OKAY IF YOU'RE NOT OKAY.

> Remember: Writing can be an escape.
> Writing can be an act of optimism.
> Writing can be an act of resistance.
> Writing can be rage, spite, power.
> It can be the way out, or the way in.
> Stories have meaning.
> Your stories matter.

EPILOGUE
You Can't Run on a Broken Leg

I TOLD MYSELF I COULD WRITE THROUGH ANYTHING.

On 9/12/2001, I wrote.

Day after my father died, I wrote.

Day after our taco terrier died, I wrote.

Writing was proof I was okay. Writing in tough times was a way forward, it was normalcy, it was order in the face of chaos. It was a middle finger to the cruelty of the universe, it was Captain America wiping blood from his mouth and getting up and then saying, "I can do this all day."

It was also, maybe, *maybe*, just a little bit of bullshit.

I mean, maybe it wasn't? Maybe it was who I was at that time and what I needed. Certainly the way I was during my Younger Writer[1] days was different from how I am now, as a Writer in the Midst of a Career, and I'll surely be different still during my Old Man Wendig Yells His Weird Stories to

---

1 Portrait of the Wendig as a Young Man.

Any Passersby Who Will Listen phase.[2] But time made me different.

Then—

In September 2019, my mother died.

This, already in the midst of political and cultural turmoil.

This, only months before we heard tell of odd pneumonia cases popping up in China, and about six months before we locked down our lives in the thrall of a global pandemic.

And, as I write this now, in September 2021, that global pandemic—COVID-19, in case you've been living under a rock[3] —is still cooking with gas.[4]

But! Ha ha, I thought, I will not be felled by such *grim news*. The world is full of grim news all of the time, certainly I shall not be knocked off my feet by the tiniest of breezes. Onward I go, oh ho, to triumph and prevail and to *write my way through all of it*, I assured myself most confidently, as I sat in front of the computer and opened up a blank page and hovered my fingers over the keyboard and then stared at it for a little while. And then a little while longer. And then just long enough to decide, "Ah, okay, sure, I just need a day," so I took the day, certain I would *get right back to it* the following day. Yet on the following day I once more stared at a blank space unbroken by writing. I gazed into that icy void, sure a story would come. A paragraph. A sentence. *One fucking word, please.*

Maybe I needed two days.

2   Though I'm really far more interested in my final phase, The Eldritch Wendig Rises from the Deep and Scribes One Last Heretical Tome in the Language of Dead Angels but Then When You Translate It and Go Mad, You Discover It's Really Just a Series of Tweets About Heirloom Apples.

3   Or on conspiracy-driven Facebook pages.

4   I'm editing this now in July 2022, and yep, still going!

Maybe a week.

A . . . month?

Except.

I didn't write anything new from September 2019 to September 2020.

One year.

One year.

One fucking year.

Fuck. Fuuuuuuuuck.

=

THERE WERE EMOTIONS.

Some days I thought, *Well, I'm not a writer anymore.* A writer writes, and I was not writing.

Some days I thought, *I'll get back there, I just need to sit here in front of the blank void and demand it speak to me. Maybe if I shake my computer like a baby.*[5]

Some days I thought, *To hell with this, I didn't want to write anyway, books are stupid, nobody reads anymore.*

Maybe I'll just take pictures of birds as my job, I decided.

Maybe I'll just be a bird.

Birds don't give a shit about our silly human problems.

I already tweet a lot, like birds do.

I'll fly around, I'll trill and warble, I'll poop on rich people's cars.

What a wonderful, carefree life. Until I fly into someone's bay window and concuss myself into a dirt-nap. Craaaaaap.

---

5   Wait, no, *don't* shake babies. See, that's why this is a book about writing and not parenting. Whew.

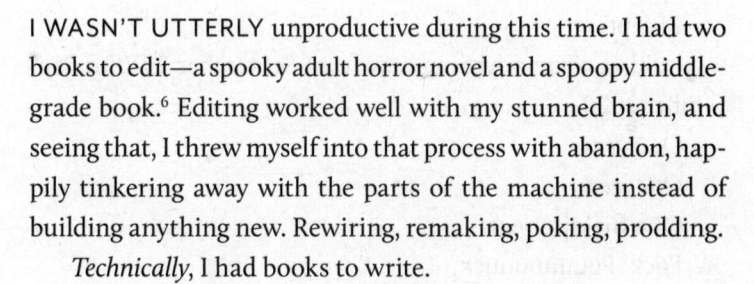

I WASN'T UTTERLY unproductive during this time. I had two books to edit—a spooky adult horror novel and a spoopy middle-grade book.[6] Editing worked well with my stunned brain, and seeing that, I threw myself into that process with abandon, happily tinkering away with the parts of the machine instead of building anything new. Rewiring, remaking, poking, prodding.

Technically, I had books to write.

But when I tried to write them—

I winced, flinched, and backed out of the room like I'd just seen a ghost. Going to write anything new was just . . . hard. Like everyone else, I suspect, I felt tired. Hollowed out. Worried all the time. Whether or not one actually feels like the world is ending,[7] there was definitely a persistent background noise of The Apocalypse. The pandemic set that to a loud, wasp-nest *hum.* There we all were, trapped in our homes. People were dying. We felt unsure who was safe, what was okay, why any of this was happening at all. There existed a handful of months where nobody knew what to do: OKAY HONEY, I'M GOING TO WEAR THIS HAZMAT SUIT AND BLEACH THESE PEARS I JUST BOUGHT, IF YOU SEE ANYBODY AT THE DOOR, THEY'RE PROBABLY A ZOMBIE AND NEED TO BE DROPPED INTO THE OUBLIETTE I BUILT ON THE FRONT STOOP. ALSO, JUST TO BE SURE, I'M GOING TO GOBBLE

---

6   *The Book of Accidents* and *Dust & Grim*, respectively, available where books are sold, unless you're reading this from some dystopian hellscape future where bookstores are extinct oh no.

7   It has certainly felt this way before, and will feel this way again, and certainly history is full of apocalypses both lowercase *a* and capital *A*.

DOWN SOME HORSE MEDICINE, BECAUSE HORSES ARE
BASICALLY PEOPLE.

It was like trauma had suffused the air. Perfuming it. If it
wasn't happening to us, it was happening to family and friends,
and also to the world at large. If you have any empathy at all,[8]
then it was quite difficult not to feel like you were pickling
yourself in the pain-and-anxiety brine of the world around you.

And it's very hard to be creative in those times.

Not impossible, of course. A number of writers I know were
able to compartmentalize and escape into the words on the
page. But just as many—if not more—felt stunted or outright
stopped by the whole affair. For some I've talked to, it felt like
tonguing a broken tooth. For others, like the well had gone dry,
like the bucket was coming up empty—no creativity[9] to be
summoned.

And what are you if you can't do the thing that you do?

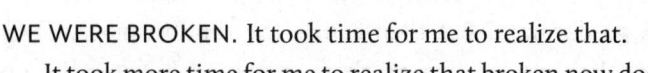

WE WERE BROKEN. It took time for me to realize that.

It took more time for me to realize that broken now doesn't
mean broken forever.

---

8   And I might argue that writers are usually creatures with an overabun-
dance of empathy, if only so we can relate to the many characters who are
very much Not Us even as they are secretly Kinda Sorta Us.

9   Originally instead of "creativity," I'd written "Muse Juice," which makes
me feel uncomfortable for reasons I cannot quite put my finger on. And yet,
I felt like including it here, in this footnote, for other reasons I cannot properly pinpoint. Anyway. Here we are, and we're all just going to have to deal
with "Muse Juice" being a thing that was typed out and printed in a book.
I'm sorry and/or you're welcome.

It took even *more* time for me to figure out that feeling this way, being this way—it was normal. It was okay. It was okay to not be okay.

=

AS NOTED, I started writing again in September 2020.

I wrote, and wrote, and wrote, and ended up finishing that book—*Wayward*, the sequel to my ha ha oops pandemic book, *Wanderers*—about nine months later.[10]

How?

How did I do it?

How did I finish it? How the hell did I even *start* writing again?

I felt injured by the times.

And so, I treated my creativity as if it were injured, too.

Treating an injury is—well, we know how you do that, for the most part. An injury means, at first, rest. Sometimes too much rest, rest that makes you (ironically) restless—you hibernate, go dormant. But then comes the time to move. Then comes the time for physical therapy: you can't just sprint on your busted leg, but you can, and must, move it. And you do this in a slow, measured way. A little at a time. Five minutes here, fifteen there, more each day. A longer walk. Soon, a run. And even in running, you set a small target: a quarter mile, then stop. Run a little, walk a lot. Eventually that flips: run a lot, walk a little. A mile. Three miles. And at that point, the injury is . . . well, maybe it's not all the way gone, but you've

---

10 Congratulations! She's a healthy, happy book baby!

learned to deal with it, it's there in your body, you've accommodated it as you can, as you must. You move. You go.

You're back.

This is all easier said than done, of course, and as a metaphor, it has its weaknesses.[11] Certainly not all injuries can be healed to a cool 100 percent. Life is complex. Our minds and bodies equally so.

Just the same, approaching it that way helped me.

I had to remember: you can't run on a broken leg.

It needs time to heal, and even when it heals, you're still going to be slow.

With *Wayward*, I wrote . . . I dunno, maybe 250 words that first day. Far below my usual *2,000 words per day* schedule. And I knew it was going to be a biggish book: *Wanderers* was 280,000 words, and as it would turn out, *Wayward* was going to be exactly the same word count. So starting slow felt daunting, impossible, like if I was going to write this book I needed to go bigger, harder, faster, right out of the gate. Wisely, I resisted this impulse. Some rare part of me is occasionally smart, and I let that smart part take the wheel.

Because the next day, I wrote 500 words.

And I did that, daily, for maybe a week.

Then I nudged it up a little, and up a little more, and a few months in, I was writing consistently a thousand words a day, sometimes two, sometimes three. It was erratic. I once upon a

---

11 No metaphor is perfect, which is why it's a metaphor. If it were perfect, it'd be something like, "The ocean was like an ocean." Which wouldn't be a metaphor. The poetry of our language is imprecise, and I believe that the joy we find in it lurks in those janky imperfections.

time had a reliably steady gait, so to speak, through a story, but ohhh not this time: some days were lost to just feeling the apocalyptic white noise again, or taking a day to experience some joy such as during the spring migration of birds,[12] or, if I'm being honest, sometimes I lost too much time staring at the blinky glowy Doom Square that is my phone. The output remained erratic, but you know what? Erratic output is still *output*. I was still doing it.

Day by day. Word by word.

And then *Wayward*, that rough beast, was born.

=

THE QUESTION THEN becomes: Why?

Why bother? The times, so uncertain, so chaotic, force us to reckon with the reality of our work, its meaning, and further, its *value*. Excuse the profanity,[13] but just what the fuck is the point? Why persevere?

It's a really important question because to answer it is to find the reason to keep going. And having no answer can very easily kneecap those efforts.

———

12 Seriously, I had one day this past year where it was Warbler Town. WHO RULE WARBLERTOWN? WARBLER ADORBLER RULE WARBLERTOWN. On that day I saw the following birds: magnolia warbler, veery, black-throated blue warbler, black-and-white warbler, common yellowthroat, yellow-rumped warbler, great crested flycatcher, northern parula, black-throated green warbler, chestnut-sided warbler, blue-headed vireo, rose-breasted grosbeak, ruby-crowned kinglet, spade-backed grovelbird, Red Shirley, Cox's Orange Pippin, and an apocalypse tanager. I may have made a few of those up. One may be an apple. Shut up.

13 Not sure why I'm asking you to excuse it *now*, at the end of the book; better to ask forgiveness than permission, one supposes.

My thoughts on this are both simple and complex.

To begin with the complex, it's because art and stories matter. Art is a multiplicative, many-headed thing: art is an act of resistance, art is an act of escape, art is a way to reckon with our reality and our anxieties, art is a way to express a message or idea or belief, and to paraphrase Margaret Atwood, art is optimism.[14] Also? You know what? Telling stories is an act not only of optimism, but of faith. It is an exhortation against being alone. It is you calling out in the dark, hoping the tale you tell will be heard by someone else—heard and loved. It's a message in a bottle, sure there's a recipient on the other side of the sea. It's this foolish, wonderful, essential entreaty that says, "I'm going to write this story that lives in my heart and somewhere out there is someone else like me, someone who has the same story-shaped hole in their heart." A mighty echo. A narrative yawp.

Stories matter. You need no further evidence of that than you are reading this book. You're reading it for a reason; some part of you wants to tell all the stories that are in your heart and your head and all your weird wiggly interstitial places. You've read books that have become a part of you. Not just novels, either—comics, TV shows, films, games, nonfiction books, articles, stories upon stories that have affected you in ways both microscopic and catastrophic. Soft, small stories. Seismic, world-altering stories. They matter to you, the writer, because

---

14   Full quote: "Anybody who writes a book is an optimist. First of all, they think they're going to finish it. Second, they think somebody's going to publish it. Third, they think somebody's going to read it. Fourth, they think somebody's going to like it. How optimistic is that?"

you are surely a reader. And they matter to the readers who will find *your* stories, too.

Though, at the simplest level, you can discard all those reasons and cleave to the purest:

You write because you jolly well fucking want to.

You write because you like it.

Because it's a part of who you are.

Because it's what you do, what you wanna keep doing, and piss on the shoes of anybody who tells you different.[15]

I think the pandemic—coupled with everything from climate change to George Floyd to the Capitol insurrection—has forced a vital recalibration upon all of us. It certainly has for me, and having spoken to other writers, it has for them, too. And it seems to have gone beyond writers: we are in the midst of the Great Resignation, where we have record numbers of people quitting their jobs, often it seems because they are underpaid, poorly treated, and do not find enough meaning in the work to justify the low pay and abuse. I don't think writing, or being a writer, is necessarily comparable in this regard, but I *do* think there is a similar search going on in our work for meaning.

This is not a thing I can confirm with data, but it feels like for a long time we've all just been trying to write whatever we can write to get that book deal, to get book sales, to please an audience. Certainly not universally—I don't mean to paint every writer with this brush. At some level we were always looking for meaning in the work too, because we were brought to

---

15   I suppose *piss on the shoes of those who oppose your art* is not a gentle notion, so feel free to reword as, "Softly micturate upon the shoes of those who wish to deny you your chance to tell stories."

the page because something in the unwritten story called to a different something inside ourselves. But now, I think, everything that's going on has parted the fog that gathered around the original purpose and clarified for us that we do want meaning in the work again. Maybe we don't want to write just to be published, but rather, we want to find something that matters—if not to The Whole World, then certainly to Our Own Damn Selves. I think that's a good thing. I think that's a kindness we can do for ourselves, too. We are all being reminded, somewhat forcefully now, that this ride we're on will end. The carousel will go 'round and 'round, but will one day start to slow, and will, without warning, stop. I don't say this to be morose, or to end on such a dire note[16] . . . but I do think there's something freeing in that reminder. It makes the moments we have matter. It gives us the urgency to write the things we want to write, whether those things are bold-facedly staring down our greatest fears and problems, or whether those things are joyfully running through an escape hatch in order to portal us and the readers to a nicer world for a time. Recognizing the reality of collapse and mortality has value. It can free you, if you let it.

It's okay if these aggregate moments in history have shaken you up. The Jenga tower maybe came down. But that's an opportunity to build it back up. With greater form and stability than before. It's a chance to remake your vision for yourself and your writing. We're beaten up, beaten down, a little bit broken, a little bit lost. That's okay. We'll find our way up and out.

---

16 *GENTLE WRITING ADVICE: HA HA WE ARE ALL GOING TO DIE.* Instant *New York Times* bestseller right there, baby.

It's okay that you're not okay. It's okay that you feel broken. Even still—

Tell your stories.

Art your art.

Go slow if you must. Be erratic. Be wild. Be you. You don't need to run. You barely need to walk. Hobbling is fine. This can be a game of inches and not miles. The story will come. You'll find your way to a new home.

Let's write.

Acknowledgments
and Afterbird

AT THE FORE OF THIS BOOK IS A DEDICATION, AND that dedication is:

This one's for the birds.

It is, of course, an attempt to be clever—and you can decide how clever it is, or isn't—because it plays two ways for me:

First, in that the phrase *for the birds* is suggestive of something silly, trivial, pure nonsense. Which is in line with what I think about writing advice despite giving you a book full of it: writing advice is very foolish, as I can't tell you how to write a book any more than I can tell you how to feel about something. And yet, here we are, reading a book in which I do exactly that. Because as much as I can't tell you how to write, I can tell you how *I* write, and the ways that *I* feel about this whole thing that we do, and maybe that is of some value to you.

Second, in that *birds* are actually a genuine part of my writing process. Sadly, this sounds way more awesome than I mean it; I do not possess princess-like powers where I trill a musical song and a pack of cartoon bluebirds descend upon my desk to write the story for me.[1] Rather, what it means is this:

Writers are very frequently in their own heads too often. At least, this is true of the writers I know, and it may be true for you, too: we live in the internal, interstitial space of our own mindscapes, and that is both the place where we start to craft our fiction and also a place in which I think we can get trapped. For as good as our mindspaces are at creating fictional scenarios about sentient robots and shadow monsters and dramatic divorces and spy chases and flouncing romances, said mindspaces can also be *just as good* at creating scenarios in which we are—well, the book covers a lot of that, doesn't it? Impostors! Failures! Fools! Poor in comparison to everyone else, doomed to dwell in obscurity, incapable of stringing together a single cogent sentence! Our minds are fertile ground for fiction both good and bad, and sometimes it's a really good idea to get *out* of our minds.

Now how one does this is up to the individual—anything from, "I listen to ASMR" to "I drop acid and yarn-bomb the town square." No judgment. You do you. That is arguably one of the very points of this book: *you do you.*

You do you, but I gotta do me,[2] and for me, the way I get out of my own head in my own way is to go look at, listen to, and occasionally photograph birds.

Now, initially, the goal would've been to leave the supposedly clever dedication alone. I mean, if I have to explain it, it's

---

1   Or, if you prefer the horror-fed version, where I sit upon my authorial Throne of Lies and vomit forth a flock of angry *word-ravens* who tear at the parchment in front of me, pecking words into it.

2   No, not like that.

really not that clever, is it? I certainly leave enough bread-crumbs about birds[3] throughout the book, which should hand-ily let you connect the dots.

And yet, here I am, explaining it.

Why? Well.

Once I started to think about the subject of birds, I felt like this was something I actually wanted to talk about, and how those *birds* help me to make *words*. Because honestly? Birding is a little bit like writing. I mean, I guess anything is if you're will-ing to stretch metaphor like Jersey Shore boardwalk taffy, but I do honestly think that some of the lessons I've taken away from birding are also lessons that can apply to writing.

So consider this one last little bit of advice—a *listicle*[4] of sorts about how birding is like writing.

1. How I Found the Birds

This isn't a piece of advice so much as a snippet of Wendigian history: when I was writing the book *Blackbirds*, I did not begin writing that book with any particular interest in birds. Birds were, to me, quite dull creatures: they're always flapping about and whistling at you, and if you don't take much time to look

---

3   Sidenote: Did you know you should not feed bread or other cereal foods to birds? Not ducks, not geese, not gulls. It's just not good for them! Bread has no nutritional value for birds, but they'll eat it (just like I will), and it'll weigh them down and stop them from getting the food they actually need (oh god also just like me).

4   *Listicle* is not a good word. It sounds lurid and scrotal, but in a spread-sheety sort of way. It's like *blog*, another similarly terrible word that we use but really, really shouldn't.

for them, you'll pretty much see: (a) robins, (b) blue jays, (c) more robins. Maybe a crow or two, and okay, fine, *they're cool*, but beyond that, birds were morning yellers and wanton car-poopers and not much else.

Titling the book after a bird was more a metaphor than anything else: the lead character's last name was Black, and blackbirds in the occult sense are psychopomps, meaning they shuttle souls from the land of the living to the realm of the dead. Appropriate, given the subject matter of a young woman who can see how you're going to die, right? But I didn't have any interest in the birds themselves.

Until I started researching them.

They're lovely birds, quite varied. Red-winged blackbird! Yellow-headed blackbird! Rusty blackbird![5] Plus there are other blackbirds that aren't even *called* blackbirds, like orioles, cow-birds, bobolinks. And you might learn that the blackbird can be victim to the parasitic cuckoo, a bird we usually know from its entanglement with fancy German clocks, but that is also a brood parasite that lays its own eggs inside the nests of other birds in order to get those other birds to help hatch their cuckoo babies. But! Cowbirds, which are blackbirds, are also brood par-asites, but whose parasitic predations are still protected by law because they're not invasive birds—unlike the house sparrow here in America, which will gladly starve a mother bird in her birdhouse nest by blocking the entrance from the male bird bringing in food, and then if the mother bird manages to lay any eggs, the house sparrow might just puncture those with its beak

---

5   Rusty Blackbird is the name I will take when I am confronted by my nemesis and forced to take a human bartending job where I will also be-come a vital patron of the local volleyball team.

before killing the mother before *building its own nest on top of the dead mother and babies* aaaahhhhh—

Anyway. What I'm saying is, birds are fascinating.

And they represented for me an accidental interest. I followed that interest and began to incorporate it into my other Miriam Black books—each is named after a different bird,[6] and I also adapted her powers to incorporate more *bird-specific horror*. So maybe there is a lesson here, and it's to find the strange threads of interest you pick up during research and tug on them to see what unravels. Because what you might end up with is something far more fascinating than you expected, and isn't that one of the great joys of writing, and of life?

2. Sometimes You Find the Bird . . .

I grew up with a father who was a hunter, and he took me hunting often. I liked the hunting and tracking part—less so the shooting and killing part. It was like, "Wow, look, we found a deer!" That was the exciting part. Not the shooting it. The finding of it. The seeing. Watching it in that moment, in nature. (No judgment against hunters; in the earlier portion of my life, we didn't have much money, and you could fill a freezer with meat from an animal like deer or elk.)

Birding is, in this way, like hunting—except for me, the only shooting I'm doing is with a DSLR camera. It is, quite

---

6   In order: *Blackbirds, Mockingbird, The Cormorant, Thunderbird, The Raptor & The Wren, Vultures*. The fact that I never got to name one of those books *Rough-Faced Shag* is still a dark spot on my career. One day, perhaps.

often, an act of pursuit: you hear a song, you spy movement, you've heard tales of a specific bird in a specific area, and so you move through that space, roving far and wide and probably putting a crick in your neck[7] because you're often looking up into the trees.

The other day, I was at a nearby Audubon sanctuary, and I heard the excitable fanboy warble of an indigo bunting—a dark blue songbird that is not necessarily uncommon on the East Coast, but one that's hard to see and that, honestly, I don't see or hear that often around here. So, upon hearing it, I ducked through the woods, trying to catch sight of it—and then it moved. It went *over there*. So *over there* I went, through the woods, to the thicket edge opening into a field, and listened for a while—*aaaaand* of course the bird had moved again, farther out this time, so across the field I went, trying not to tromp about like the clumsy oafs we humans are. Suddenly, I heard the bird dead ahead of me, in a copse of trees and understory. And it was there I stood for like fifteen fucking minutes, going cross-eyed trying to find this small dark blue bird in the dark green leaves and dark tangle. The bird's fast-pitched trill was like a taunt. HA HA, YOU CAN'T FIND ME, AND YET HERE I AM, SINGING MY HEART OUT.

And then! It *moved*. Just a little. Flitting from one branch to the next. And I managed to snap a couple pics before the bird spotted me spotting it and took off for another fencerow somewhere else. I heard like six more indigo buntings then all

---

7   Aka, "Warbler Neck." Which is not a town in upstate New York, but rather the condition during spring or fall migration where you stare upward for minutes on end trying to spy a tiny mouse-sized bird bopping along branches behind like a million leaves.

around me, a surround-sound chorus of bird taunts, and I couldn't see a one of them—but I had a shot, and I went home, satisfied in the thrill of the hunt.

So how is this like writing?

Because sometimes the idea, the story, needs chasing. It is not enough to let it be what it is when you first hear it or detect signs of it. It must be hounded, developed, you must pursue it. Stories can be an act of pursuit in this way, and that is why writing is sometimes like work. It necessitates tromping across a field, or darting through the thorn-tangle bramble to get not just *a* shot, but to get *the* shot—meaning, to tell the story as it must be told, not a half-hearted, half-baked, half-assed attempt. I am keen to caution folks not to give stories too much power, too much magic, for at the end of the day we must be in charge of them—and yet, it is hard not to sometimes realize that it very much *feels* like they are in charge of us, that they can be tricky, that they can evade us, that they are living things made of very real magic and it is on us to hunt them to wherever they hide.

3. . . . Sometimes the Bird Finds You

Similar situation, just the other day: For about three days, I was hearing a pair of American redstarts[8] in my yard. And for those three days, I chased them around said yard, capturing only fleeting glimpses of these little birds up in the trees,

---

8   If you don't know what an American redstart is, think "squishier kawaii version of a Baltimore oriole." The male, at least, is mostly black, but with some notable patches of glorious orange. It is also a bird with a small beak and an incredulous stare. It is judging you, even now.

resulting in photos that were not unlike any photo you've seen of Bigfoot. All I got were blurry, smeary streaks of bird-shadow and not much more.

But I was doing the work. I was listening. I was looking. I was pursuing.

And then—

Day three. I had mostly given up. I assumed the birds had migrated on, as they do—they're usually only here for a week or less, and then they fuck off to whatever bird party they're late for, presumably.

I was standing at the edge of the yard, not far from the road, trying to find a bird and not seeing any or hearing any—

And directly in front of me, in the hedge, the male American redstart popped up. So close that I had to dial my zoom lens all way down to even get a shot in focus. And there the bird hung out for a few minutes, singing, chirping, and casting its judgmental stare my way as if to say, I HEARD YOU WERE LOOKING FOR ME, HUMAN. WELL, HERE I AM. SAY YOUR PIECE, YOU PINK, FEATHERLESS GOOSE. I WILL TAKE YOUR MESSAGE TO THE AVIAN SATRAPY FOR CONSIDERATION. I of course had no message except *please don't move*, because I was getting some very good photos.

Eventually the bird left, and was gone, and I haven't seen any of them since.

But I got the shot.

And I did almost nothing to get that shot except stand there like the pink featherless goose that I am.

So that's the other lesson:

Sometimes writing isn't pursuit. Sometimes writing is waiting. Sometimes it isn't about moving forward or chasing an idea—sometimes it is simply the act of standing still. Sometimes, we hunt for inspiration—we hound the Muse across the field and forests. Other times? The goddess just shows up, unbidden. Or, put differently, we have to be willing to stand there like a pink featherless goose.

Here you're surely like, "But you just said we have to hunt the ideas, we have to do the work," and yes, that's true. But the opposite thing is true, too. Which is perhaps more the point of this: Writing is not one thing. Our process is not codified and easily repeatable. What worked before may not work this time. Every story is different and every writer of every story is different—even the same writer is a different writer next time they write. It's just how it is. And it's why again and again I attempt to remind you through this book that writing advice is useful, yes, but it is never, ever[9] meant to be gospel. Writing advice cannot accurately capture the myriad ways of telling a story and living the writing life any more than you can capture a bolt of lightning with your bare hands.

Sometimes you hunt the bird.

Sometimes the bird hunts you.

So it is with words, as well as with birds.

4. Look Around, Unfocus Your Eyes

With birds, you don't know what you're going to find when you look around. It's a simple thing, but utterly essential: You are in field or forest or even in a city park, look around. Look up. Look

---

9   EVER.

down. Look mid-tree, look at the reeds around a pond, look in the hedge. You don't know what you'll see. You'll probably see a bird or three, and that's quite exciting.

Further, when you do look around, there is a trick I find where I'm less looking for birds than I am looking for . . . the general *presence* of birds. Finding a bird in a tree is a far more wearying game than Where's Waldo—birds are designed to hide in the trees. Yellow warblers are just the perfect color of the sun coming through the new spring leaves—and they're often quite small. So what you end up looking for is not exactly the bird itself but signs of its passing: you're looking for the moving of the bird dancing between branches, you're looking for the shaking of leaves where there might be a bird trying to snatch up a caterpillar snack, you're looking for the shape of a nest.

Of course, you never know if you're going to be looking at the right spot at the right time, because what are the chances that you're focusing in on the perfect square foot of reality in a theoretical infinity of square feet? Who knows? You sure don't. I don't, either.

So what I do is, I unfocus my eyes. I let them sort of . . . go blurry. It's like looking at those Magic Eye posters, trying to find the laser dolphin or whatever it is. You kinda *zone out* a little bit. And in removing a lot of the visual specificity, you end up seeing things in your periphery: you catch the movement, you spot the subtle changes that suggest *birdsign*. Sometimes you see the bird by looking for everything but the bird.

Now how is this useful in writing?

Looking around is obviously quite useful because our stories are often the result of a brain-based algorithm sorting through and contextualizing all the things we've seen and experienced. We need input to create output. We need to feed our brains information, and so we must look around to gather that information—this can mean whatever it is you want it to mean, of course. It can mean doing a lot of nonspecific research. I love nonfiction for this: fiction gives me a fiction writer's idea, but nonfiction always gives me my *own* ideas. But it can also mean checking out books and even the internet, and it can mean, just as it does with birding, going out into the world. See some stuff. Watch people. Examine buildings, furniture, trees, birds. Go to a zoo. Go to a forest. Walk in a field. Eat something weird at a restaurant. Give yourself input.

In terms of *unfocusing your eyes*—that, too, helps writing, if you understand it metaphorically. Giving yourself input and finding stories doesn't always mean viewing the world explicitly as a pile of resources for your writing. You go to look at the world (its nature, its people, its everything) *not* with the explicit, specific goal of fueling your work, but rather just to be in the moment and to experience those things. And then, oddly enough, you often fuel the work and find the story *anyway*. Sometimes, finding the story is an act of zoning out—and that can involve anything from traveling the globe to mowing the lawn. It's about tuning part of your world out to make room for the stories to come in. Sometimes you find the bird by not looking for the bird. Sometimes you find the story by not looking for the story.

5. Take the Adventure

A special note, too, about traveling:

Sometimes, to find the interesting birds, you have to travel.

I do not mean simply in a specific area: "Oh, there's a bird over there." I mean, you have to drive a half hour to a bird sanctuary. Or you have to get on a plane and go a state away, or across the country, or across the world. Travel that is local, domestic, or international will allow you to see NEW BIRDS, and so it is with writing and storytelling. Sometimes, for new input, we have to travel. A short drive, a long train trip, an epic flight. Whatever you can manage, whatever you can afford. Leave your house. Go somewhere else.

It is there that you will find the birds, and often, the words.

6. You Need the Right Tools

Birding requires a few tools. Not many. But some, such as: a way to see at a distance (binoculars, zoom lens), maybe some boots, possibly a map, a little bug spray to thwart pernicious ticks and skeeters, also a giant bird costume because that is how you let the birds know you are SAFE and ONE OF THEM.

Wording, too, requires a few tools. Not many. But some, such as: research tools, a computer that won't catch fire, a word processor of reasonable repute, maybe an outline if you're that kind of writer, also a giant bird costume because the very best writers write while wearing a giant bird costume.[10]

Also, bring snacks. When looking at birds, or writing words.

---

10   Margaret Atwood is known to dress as a hooded merganser when writing her exquisite novels! Probably!

7. Sometimes We Leave the Nice Birds Alone

The goal of birding is to observe, not to disrupt. To celebrate the birds, not to climb up into their nest and sit on their eggs.

And though I'd note that quite often, storytelling is very much an act of disruption—at the same time, sometimes stories are observances. They're not us making a case for anything, they're not about us stomping about with big footprints or levying judgment. And sometimes we just need to leave them alone to let them be what they're going to be.

8. Some Days You Don't See Anything

I've had many a birding day where I don't see anything. I mean, okay, it's a rare day where I literally see no birds—I have not yet experienced a kind of BIRDPOCALYPSE. Even in a Walmart parking lot you're going to see a crow or a sea gull or something, and there are thankfully vultures[11] often wheeling about in the sky on their invisible axes. I only mean, not every day is a WOW WHIZBANG WHOADANG birding day. And not every wording day is, either. And that's all right. You go in, you put the words down, even if not every day feels like you're seeing a cerulean warbler or a scarlet tanager or a North Scranton judgment wren. Some days are for horses, not unicorns, and that's okay.

---

11 Vultures are good and essential birds and we must protect them. They also can use their vomit as a weapon and pee on themselves to cool off. Vultures are awesome.

9. You Don't Need to Know What You're Doing

If you want to go birding, you can just start.

If you want to be a writer, you can just start.

You don't need to have special skills.

You just go and do the thing.

You'll develop skills. You'll figure out habits and patterns. You'll know what happens if you bird in the morning versus the evening, and you'll also see what it's like when you write in the morning or the evening. You'll get a sense for why you do it, why you like it, what is satisfying to you. You'll find your routines, your favorite spots, then you'll become too married to them and switch it up. If the birds stop showing up to your usual places, you'll find new places. And if your process no longer produces words, you'll find a new process.

But to begin, you just begin.

You find the birds.

You find the words.

10. Sometimes It's About the Escape

The world is a hard place. Maybe easier now than it was a century before, but it is now—and likely in every generation—a complicated, troubling, traumatic place. We want it to be full of love, and sometimes it is, but a lot of times, it is not.

And so we seek escape.

Birding can be escape. It can be an escape from our own bad brains, it can be an escape from whatever horror show is going on around us.

But writing can be an escape, too. For you and for the readers. It doesn't have to be. Writing can just as easily be an act of confrontation—a place to go to summon the demons of this age and hit them with sticks. But even when it's that, writing is always a step removed—it's a conjured realm where we can go and grapple with these things, these problems, these ideas.

It's okay to find escape.

We often treat "escape" like it's a dirty word, but it is in this escape that we can find both peace and truth. I've found a lot of peace—and a lot of truth—while standing out in a forest listening to and looking for birds. And I have found the same measure of peace and truth when sitting at a keyboard, listening to my thoughts and looking for ways to catalyze and crystallize them onto the page. Whether in a story, in a blog post, or in a book such as this one.

And Now, the Actual Acknowledgments

I thank the birds, obviously, though they won't read this book.[12] I also thank every writer, both young and old, published and not, who has ever read the silly things I say about writing and shared them with others—it's quite nice and I always appreciate it. Margaret Atwood in particular is deserving of special thanks—as of this writing she still recommends my blog, *Terribleminds*, on her own website, which continues to shock me and would certainly be a thing I'd tell myself if I could go

---

12 They have much better taste.

back in time about twenty-five years.[13] I also thank my editor of this book, Lauren Appleton, who I suspect is my editor because her last name contains the word "apple," another thing that, like birds, I like quite a lot. And special thanks as always to my agent, Stacia Decker, who has been with me since the first novel and I hope will be my agent to the last.

I suspect this will be my last writing book, in part because the older I get and the more I write, the less I actually know, and so in three years the only kind of writing advice I'll be able to offer you is a tapestry of the words I HAVE NO FUCKING IDEA WHAT I'M DOING written over and over again in Comic Sans. Certainly as my own process changes and squirms about, I continue to disagree with my own writing advice, to the point I probably already disagree with something I've said in this very book. Which sounds like a problem, but I actually think it's quite a good thing: writing and giving advice about writing is a conversation, not a declaration. It's a dialogue about how we do this thing, and in dialogue, there is never just one side chatting with itself in agreement, but rather, there is agitation. And agitation is good. Agitation stirs creativity. Little burrs and thorns of disagreement and uncertainty are what keep us moving forward in a persistent act of consideration and reconsideration of what we do, how we do it, and most curious of all, *why* we do it.

Thanks of course too to all of you who have procured this book in some fashion. I hope it helped you in some small, strange way.

Be well. Stay safe. Write on.

---

13 For posterity, what she says on her website is, "Some writers self-publish successfully. Many don't. Take advice. You will find a lot of good practical tips (and swear words) on www.terribleminds.com."

About the Author

Photograph of the author by Michelle Wendig

Chuck Wendig is the *New York Times* bestselling author of *Wanderers*, *The Book of Accidents*, and *Wayward*, and over two dozen other books for adults and young adults. A finalist for the Astounding Award and an alum of the Sundance Screenwriters Lab, he has also written for comics, games, and film/television. He's known for his popular blog, *Terribleminds*, and his books about writing, such as *Damn Fine Story*. He lives in Bucks County, Pennsylvania, with his family.